You're Hired!

A Nurse's Guide to Success in Today's Job Market

By Brenda Brozek, MAOL, RN

Cover design by Jessica Bloom
Content design by Dena Fisher
Illustrations by Elizabeth Brozek

Foreword by Patricia McFarland, MS, RN, FAAN

Produced by California Nursing Students' Association
Endorsed by Association of California Nurse Leaders

You're Hired! A Nurses Guide To Success In Today's Job Market

Published by:
California Nursing Students' Association
2520 Venture Oaks Way, Suite 210
Sacramento, CA 95833
www.cnsa.org

To order additional books, buy in bulk, order for corporate use, request a review copy for course adoption, request author information or for speaker or other media requests, contact the California Nursing Students' Association at (916) 779-6949, or info@acnl.org.

ISBN-13: 978-1-4507-3845-3

Printed in the United States of America by Paul Baker Printing

To my husband, John! Your love and encouragement support me in all my endeavors.

And to our mentors...where would we be without them?

Acknowledgements

I am very grateful to the following people who helped make this book a reality:

Patricia McFarland, your wisdom, advice and guidance were critical to the success of this project.

Members of the CNSA Board, thank you for your suggestions and feedback throughout the writing of *You're Hired!*

Jessica Bloom, once again you created an eye-catching design - this time for our book cover.

Dena Fisher, thank you for stepping in to design the book contents. Your efforts kept the project on time.

Elizabeth Brozek, your creative illustrations and ideas added so much to this book.

Kay Evans, as always, your insights are of great value to me.

Elaine Nisterchuk, your proofreading and editing skills were much appreciated.

Andrew Brozek, your expertise in answering my computer questions once again bailed me out of technological hot water.

The Chico gals - Colleen, Denise, Gail, Heidi, Julie and Lauren: your encouragement was the main impetus to begin this project.

Table of Contents

Foreword

You're Hired! Two of the most exciting words I've ever heard.

My first role in health care was as a 19-year old nursing assistant in a faith-based community hospital. That was nearly 40 years ago.

Much later, I was Director of Nursing at a hospital within that same faith-based system. During a Joint Commission visit, surveyors asked to review my employment file. To my surprise, the last page of the file was a hand-written note from that original interview. All it said was: "Nice girl, cute smile—hire!"

Since then, employment rules have changed, hiring practices refined and nurse leaders have become experts at identifying and selecting outstanding registered nurses.

Yet, given the tremendous number of applicants today's nurse managers must consider when filling open positions, you are probably asking yourself: *what makes an applicant stand out?*

It's not the quality of paper the resume is printed on. Nor is it the number of emails or phone messages left by an applicant. Instead it's the demonstrated professionalism, compassion, enthusiasm and commitment that transcends the resume, application and actual interview. It is what the potential employer sees, hears, reads and <u>feels</u> when looking for the job candidate who is the best "fit" for their organization.

Brenda Brozek has provided new graduates and experienced nurses with a recipe for success. ***You're Hired!*** is a practical easy-to-read guide that will help you navigate today's stormy job market and hear those two wonderful words: *"You're Hired!"*

A number of years ago, I was preparing to testify before a very important senate committee about the nursing shortage. I was more nervous than usual, so my husband volunteered to drive me to the airport. As I stepped out of the car, he gave me this advice: "speak from your heart and you will be a success."

Employers are seeking individuals with a passion for excellence in patient care. Your instructors, mentors and coaches have prepared you well. You have the drive to succeed as a registered nurse. As you prepare for that interview, follow the key points outlined in this book and always remember to speak from your heart!

Patricia L. McFarland, MS, RN, FAAN
Chief Executive Officer, Association of California Nurse Leaders
Executive Officer, California Nursing Students' Association

Introduction

Learning To Market Yourself

"Apply the vision of what is possible and what can make it possible."

Marla Salmon, ScD, RN, FAAN

You are a unique person with your own skills, talents and abilities. You know in your heart that you are a good nurse. But how do you convey that information to potential employers? How can you convince them to hire you, instead of other candidates who are competing for the job—some with more experience and/or education than you?

How do you show them who you really are, and what you have to offer?

That's what this book is all about. Helping you to recognize your unique talents and abilities, identify the needs of potential employers and effectively communicate how you meet those needs. It's about learning to market and promote yourself. These principles apply to all nurses seeking jobs—whether it's your first job as a new graduate, or you're an experienced nurse who is seeking new employment opportunities. Learning these basic skills will serve you well throughout your career.

The unfortunate truth in the health care marketplace is that there are many more qualified applicants than available positions. The individual who gets the job is the one who best communicates his or her qualifications through their cover letter, resume and job interview.

As nurses, we are often very humble people who chose our profession out of a genuine desire to help others. The thought of "tooting our own horns" in order to promote ourselves can feel very unnatural. Many of us are uncomfortable talking about our achievements and talents. We believe actions speak louder than words. Some of us even think that talking about our accomplishments is arrogant and inappropriate.

This couldn't be farther from the truth! There is nothing arrogant or wrong about honestly and genuinely conveying your abilities, accomplishments and talents in order to secure the job that's right for you. Having a job that's a good fit is a positive for you and your employer. You'll be happier and more successful, and your employer will have a dedicated, contributing team member.

In a competitive job market, you must be willing and able to describe your abilities to potential employers, rather than hoping they'll recognize your potential and give you the job. Think of this as a contest—and you want to win first prize!

Marketing Yourself

The principles of basic marketing are: identify the needs of your customer and show them how your product fulfills those needs. The starting point is a thorough understanding of the attributes of your product. Next, comes an assessment of your potential customers. What are their needs? Does your product meet those needs? If your product meets the needs of a certain group—then those are your new customers. To close the deal, you need to help them realize, through positive communication strategies, that your product is just what they need.

These same basic principles hold true when searching for a job. Identify the employer's needs and show them how your qualifications and abilities meet those needs. You must do this in every step of the process—whether you're writing your resume and cover letter, communicating with the nurse recruiter or human resources department, preparing for the job interview or writing a thank you note following the interview.

Earlier, I mentioned honestly portraying your skills and abilities. That's where your communication strategy will differ from product advertisers and marketers. If you've ever compared an actual Big Mac to the one pictured on billboards and advertisements, you know what most consumers know—product advertisers often exaggerate the attributes and benefits of what they're trying to sell. This is where your strategy will differ. As a job seeker, it's imperative that you are honest about your qualifications. All employers verify licensure, and often check certifications and other information that you provide. It's tempting in a tough job market to exaggerate your qualifications to give you a better chance at landing the position. But, this is a dangerous game to play. Job offers have been rescinded and new employees terminated because they misrepresented themselves on their resume and/or in the job interview.

Don't underestimate the value of honesty, integrity, enthusiasm and the skills and talents you possess. Throughout this book, you'll learn how to recognize and best communicate your strengths. I'll also offer suggestions about how to build your experience.

When looking for a job, it's easy to become focused on yourself. What does XYZ Hospital have to offer me? Can I get the shift that fits my lifestyle? How much will I get paid? What training and advancement opportunities are there for me? These are all valid questions that must be answered before accepting a job offer.

The problem is, many job applicants only concentrate on the "me" side of the equation. In the competitive marketplace, successful candidates also focus on the needs of their potential employers. You must remember—it's not just about "me." It's about "us."

Employer + Me = Us

In the pages that follow, I'll show you how to demonstrate to your potential employer that your focus is on the "us." As you go through this book, you'll learn to:

- **Recognize Your Unique Skills, Talents and Abilities** - As you begin your job quest, ask yourself: What sets me apart from others? What makes me the nurse they should hire for this position?

- **Identify the Needs of Your Potential Employer** - This can include: level of clinical competence required, mission and values of the organization, organizational culture, unique patient needs, etc.

- **Communicate how Your Qualifications Meet the Employer's Needs** - This includes learning to tailor your message based on the needs of the potential employer.

• **Find Jobs and Organizations that are the Right Fit for You**
  Are your values, goals, needs and preferences in alignment
  with the potential employer's?

We will examine these principles more in-depth in subsequent
chapters. Although these strategies can be applied to other
industries, this book was written specifically for nurses—whether
you're a new graduate nurse or an experienced RN. All the
scenarios and stories you'll read are true, and occurred in a variety
of health care settings. Frequently asked questions you'll see are
based on issues and queries made during workshops and seminars
I've conducted.

This book is designed as a resource for you. It's meant to be
used over and over again to help you develop the skills to advance
your professional nursing career. Application of these strategies will
position you for success in your job search—today and in the future.

I wish you much success and happiness in your nursing career!

What Employers are Looking for in Job Candidates

"There are few, if any, jobs in which ability alone is sufficient. Needed also are loyalty, sincerity, enthusiasm and team play."

William B. Given, Jr.

Although specific needs of each organization will vary, in general, most potential employers look for similar skills and qualities in the nurses they hire. This chapter will give you an overview of the basic skills, abilities and attributes important to hiring managers.

Professional Competence

This includes basic traits and work habits for all successful employees:

- Dependability and reliability—showing up for work on time each day, working hard to get the job done and collegiality with fellow staff members at all levels.

- Loyalty to employer—saying positive things about your employer, looking for ways to improve service, positive attitude about your job and an interest in building tenure with the organization.

- Willingness to improve performance and skills—does the job candidate have a genuine desire to learn, improve and grow, rather than being satisfied with the status quo?

Professional and Clinical Competence

What are employers looking for when hiring registered nurses?
As this illustration depicts, most employers are seeking RNs with
a solid foundation of professional and clinical competence; strong
skills in communications, customer service and team collaboration;
and a commitment to the mission and vision of the organization.

Clinical Competence

This is the foundation of your nursing practice. You must possess the basic competencies for RNs, including: clinical knowledge, technical skills and critical thinking ability. The level of your clinical ability will vary depending on your years of experience as an RN. An employer will expect a higher level of clinical expertise from a ten-year RN, than they would from a recent graduate. Many employers are willing to provide additional training for those who have the characteristics they're looking for.

Recognizing Potential in Job Applicants

When I was a floor nurse, I participated on an interview panel for my nursing department. We were in the middle of the nursing shortage, and my unit was hiring six RNs and four nursing assistants. Our department manager was leading the panel. One of the candidates for the nursing assistant position was a first semester nursing student with some volunteer experience in a skilled nursing facility. What struck us most was his enthusiasm for patient care and his strong desire to become a nurse. However, there were other candidates who had much more work experience as nursing assistants. When some of the panel members pointed this out, the manager replied: "Sometimes you have to look beyond where the person is today, and try to envision where they will be in the future."

So we hired him.

And she was right! He was a very hard working and compassionate nursing assistant, who later became a much needed monitor tech and then after graduation, an exceptional RN on our unit. Today, he is the manager of a large nursing unit within the organization.

Successful hiring managers are skilled at recognizing potential and developing strategies to nurture and grow those gifts and talents.

Communication Skills

RNs must interact with patients, families, physicians, colleagues and other staff members on a regular basis. Often this communication can be in stressful situations. In July 2008, the Joint Commission issued a *Sentinel Event Alert* warning that disruptive behavior and poor communication on the part of health care team members jeopardizes patient safety. Disruptive behavior, poor communication and inability of team members to resolve conflict also affects employee retention rates and job satisfaction.

It's become increasingly clear to employers that to be successful, RNs must have excellent communication skills, including the ability to resolve conflicts in a positive manner.

Team Skills

In health care, very few employees work in isolated positions. RNs are integral members of the health care team. Successful RNs are good team players. Attributes of effective team members include:

- Ability to collaborate with others to accomplish tasks and achieve goals

- Offering assistance to other team members and asking for help when needed

- Honesty, openness and tact in communications

Customer Service

Nurses provide patient-centered care 24/7. Organizations hire RNs who understand that patients/clients/customers are their primary focus. This is especially important in today's environment where numerous websites rank hospitals on many factors, including patient satisfaction. Hospitals and their customers take these rankings very seriously. Potential patients will often use these comparison websites to shop for hospitals. As a result, employers seek staff members who are assets in building a positive reputation for their health care organizations.

Mission and Values

Most employers want staff who share and practice the mission, vision and values of their organizations. These are the employees most likely to have a long and mutually beneficial tenure with the organization.

As you can see, clinical competence isn't the only attribute employers are considering when filling open positions. In fact, an RN who is clinically competent, but a poor team player or a disruptive force on the unit, isn't an asset. Employers are looking for nurses who will be a positive force in patient care and the work environment.

When an employer considers hiring you, they're not just looking at your nursing experience. They are also evaluating your communication skills, your ability to collaborate with others, your expertise and willingness to deliver safe, compassionate care and whether you'd be a good fit for their team. Some health care organizations conduct behavioral testing to identify potential employees with the attributes they're looking for.

So don't be discouraged if you are a recent graduate and have little or no health care work experience. Employers also try to gauge the candidate's potential when making hiring decisions. Lack of clinical experience can be overcome with time, training and nurturing. Ineffective communication, poor team skills and lack of motivation are much more difficult to rectify.

And potential employers know this...

The Bottom Line

When hiring, most employers are looking for more than just health care work experience. They want nurses who are motivated, compassionate, good communicators and collaborative team players.

Finding the Organization that's Right for You

2

"Choose a job you love, and you'll never have to work a day in your life!"

Confucius

Finding a health care organization that's a good fit for you is a key factor for your success and happiness in your nursing career. Employers strive to hire workers who are well suited for their organizations. Studies have shown that employee contentment correlates with productivity, job retention and customer/patient satisfaction. There are many factors to consider when determining if a hospital or health care organization is right for you. These include: organizational culture, mission and values, organizational policies and practices, communication and teamwork among co-workers, and clinical focus.

This chapter will help you determine what's important to you when looking for potential employers. Answering the questions on the following pages will assist you in identifying your values and preferences. There are no right or wrong answers to these questions—they are a guide designed for your personal use.

My Story

When I was a nursing student, I lived around the corner from a hospital. I was born in this neighborhood hospital and it was a fixture in my life as I was growing up. Throughout nursing school, I had no other aspirations than to work in this hospital. Even though I had very positive clinical experiences in other facilities, I refused to even consider the possibility of working anywhere else after graduation.

In my final semester, I arranged to complete my last practicum in this hospital. This would set me up perfectly to transition to a job with the organization upon graduation.

To my growing dismay, I soon discovered during my practicum that the organizational culture was uncomfortable for me. The attitudes toward patient care and team communication were much different from my own views. In addition, I didn't agree with some of the hospital policies and practices.

I had to admit to myself that the only reason I wanted to work in this hospital was because it was in my neighborhood. When I analyzed all the other factors, I realized I wouldn't be happy there.

I finished my practicum and never applied for a job at my neighborhood hospital. Instead, I accepted employment at a hospital that was a much better fit. I stayed in the organization for 17 years. I'll always be glad I looked beyond my neighborhood hospital to find the organization that best fit my values, beliefs and work ethic.

How do You Determine What's Right for You?

Your first step is to examine your own values, beliefs and preferences. By learning more about yourself, you'll be better able to determine which organizations are the best matches for you. Use the questions on the following pages to help you zero in on what's important to you.

The Bottom Line

Seek employment situations that are a good fit for you. This will be a major contributor to your success and happiness in your nursing career.

Assessment Tool #1 - **Determining My Preferences**

Location

Am I willing to relocate?

Which locations do I prefer?
Rural
Medium-sized city
Large city
Suburb

Patient Care/Hospital Environment

Do I want to be in a highly specialized area, or be more generalized and care for a variety of patient types?
If you prefer a highly specialized area, you should begin your search with large hospitals. If you want to care for a variety of patients, a small hospital and/or rural setting may be best.

What size hospital would I prefer?

Do I prefer: rural or urban hospital settings?

Do I want to be on the cutting edge of research?
If yes, then consider large teaching and research hospitals.

Do I prefer a teaching environment where members of the health care team are at various stages of their training? Or do I want to work in a community hospital where most of the physicians are in private practice?

Do I want to be part of a system where I can have many avenues open to me? Or, would I prefer working for an independent hospital?
In order to compete in today's marketplace, many hospitals are part of a system. As a result, there currently aren't many hospitals operating independently. Being part of a system gives the hospital more financial power. However, the hospital must abide by the rules and policies of that system. There are usually more opportunities and benefits for employees in large systems.

What areas of nursing practice would I consider at this point?

Acute Care	Public Health
Community Health	Federal or State Agencies
Post Acute	Home Health
Hospital Based Distinct Part	Corrections
Hospice	Free Standing SNF
School Nursing	Adult Day Care
Acute Rehabilitation	Emergency Medical System
Outpatient Services	Surgery Centers
Clinics	Physician's Offices

Other areas of practice:

Which patient care unit types do I prefer?

Medical	Respiratory
Cardiac	Surgical
Maternal/Child	Critical Care
Neurology	Pediatrics
Peri-Operative	Other areas:

Commitment and Values

What is my personal philosophy regarding my role and responsibilities as a nurse?

Would I prefer my employer to be:

For Profit

Nonprofit

Government Agency

Do I want to be in a union or nonunion environment?

What type of patients do I want to serve?

Are there specific services I believe all patients should have access to?

Are there procedures I wouldn't feel comfortable being performed on my unit? At my hospital?

Are my values best aligned with a faith-based hospital environment?

If yes, which faith-based organizations best fit my values?

Training and Education

What opportunities would be best for me?

Residency program

Access to continuing education opportunities

New graduate program

Staff development department within the organization

Flexible orientation period

Tuition reimbursement

When do I plan to go back to school for an advanced degree?
Which employers support education through tuition reimbursement and flexibility of work hours?

Other Areas of Importance to Me

Use this space to list other factors that are important to you in finding the job and employer best suited for you, such as geographic environment, proximity to home, friends and family.

Hunting for Open Positions

"I'm a great believer in luck, and I find the harder I work, the more I have of it!"

Thomas Jefferson

You're ready to enter the job market and search for the position that's right for you. But how do you locate open positions? How can you rise above the competition to be noticed by potential employers? We will explore several strategies in this chapter.

Organizational Websites

The vast majority of health care organizations post open positions on their websites. This is an excellent place to start. You can view job openings, learn about minimum qualification requirements, gather information about the organization and discover who to contact for more information.

On many company websites, you also have the ability to upload your resume and request to be notified by e-mail of new positions, such as RN jobs in critical care, or entry-level RN positions for new graduates. You'll also apply for jobs through these websites.

The Power of Networking

In today's digital age, where it's so easy to shoot off resumes to multiple employers, the power of networkng is often overlooked by job candidates. Networking continues to be a key factor in successfully locating and securing nursing positions.

The following sections describe opportunities to develop and foster networks to help you land a nursing position. Building professional relationships will help you not only with your job search, but also throughout your career.

Be Prepared to Network

Always keep your resume updated so that if you make a connection with someone who can aid in your job search, you can send them a copy as soon as possible - while the connection is still fresh.

Also consider creating a business card. Not every situation is conducive to handing someone your resume. Carry cards with you at all times, since you never know when an opportunity for networking might arise. Depending on the circumstances, it may be much more appropriate to give the person you're connecting with one of your business cards.

Online printers may offer better prices than local print shops. Look for quality as well as the best deal when printing your business cards.

What should you include on your business card? Start with your name and contact information. If you're an experienced nurse, then include your credentials and perhaps your specialty area of practice. If you're a nursing student, incllude your expected graduation date. You may want to incorporate a graphic or design on the front of your business card. Printers often have templates and graphics you can use. You can also utilize the back of the card to list special skills and abilities, a statement of your philosophy regarding nursing or any other information you think will help you market yourself. **Be creative!**

Nurse Recruiters

Many health care employers utilize recruiters to market their organizations to potential employees, identify high quality job candidates and facilitate the hiring process. In small organizations, there may be only one recruiter for a variety of job roles. In large organizations, there are often several recruiters with one or more dedicated to nursing.

Some recruiters are RNs. Many are not. Don't discount recruiters because they aren't nurses. Recruiters can be powerful allies in your job search. They are the gatekeepers to the hiring managers. They can open doors for you—or they can keep them closed!

Not only are recruiters very knowledgeable about available positions, they are often aware of upcoming openings that are not yet posted. Additionally, a good recruiter knows the style and preferences of managers within the organization. Because of this, they can help you identify jobs that are a good fit for your personality, skills and needs.

Building a solid relationship with a recruiter can be a huge asset. Even if there are currently no jobs available, they will be on the lookout for future jobs that match your skills and abilities. If the facility is part of a health system, the recruiter may refer you to another hospital within the system that has an opening more suitable for you. They'll often introduce you to the recruiter at this facility, giving you an advantage over other competitors.

How do I Build a Positive Relationship with a Nurse Recruiter?

Contact them initially by telephone. Be respectful of their time—ask if this is a good time to talk. If no, make an appointment to meet with them in person or by telephone (face-to-face is better). If they are willing to talk now—tell them that you're interested in learning more about RN positions in their organization. They'll often ask a few questions. Be prepared to briefly talk about yourself and your qualifications. Ask if you can take a tour of the facility, especially the departments you're interested in. If there are no current open positions, request that they keep your resume on file. Check in periodically by telephone or e-mail.

If you're still in nursing school, don't wait until you graduate to build relationships with recruiters. As described above—contact the recruiter, make an appointment to talk and ask for a tour. Tell them when you're graduating and what nursing departments you're interested in. Perhaps they have nursing assistant positions available. This would be an excellent way to gain entry into the organization as a student.

Ask for advice about how you can strengthen your skills prior to graduation. This may include volunteer work or obtaining certifications, such as Advanced Cardiac Life Support (ACLS), Pediatric Life Support (PALS) or arrhythmia recognition (in many health care organizations, this certification makes you eligible for an employment opportunity as a monitor technician).

Some recruiters may tell you not to contact them until you've graduated. Although you want to respect their wishes, you can send them periodic e-mails to let them know about your progress. When you do enter the job market, that recruiter will hopefully recognize your name when they see your job application. This persistence may land you an interview, and ultimately a job!

Make an Appointment Before Visiting the Recruiter

Don't "stop by" to see a recruiter if you don't have an appointment. Instead, telephone them and request an appointment. Always ask: Is this a good time to talk? The recruiter will appreciate your manners and consideration. People usually remember those who treat them positively.

Always dress professionally when visiting Human Resources, the recruiter or any other person or department within the organization. Remember—every contact with a potential employer, no matter how quick or insignificant it may seem, is an opportunity to make an impression—either positive or negative.

Make sure the impression you leave is always positive!

Human Resources Department

If a health care organization doesn't have a recruiter, that role usually falls to staff in the Human Resources department. Because HR staff have other duties besides recruitment functions, they usually aren't as attuned to the nuances of specific nursing departments and job roles as a nurse recruiter would be. However, they can still be a valuable resource and help you gain access to hiring managers.

Additionally, since job applications are usually submitted online, most HR departments have computers available for use by potential employees who don't normally have access to this technology.

Career Fairs

Health Care Career Fairs are designed to match job applicants with available positions. This is also a good opportunity to meet recruiters. Pick up their business cards and later contact them as described in the previous section. This also gives you a context with which to start the conversation: "I met you at the Career Fair last week and I was just following up on our discussion…" In addition to recruiters, some employers also send RNs to Career Fairs. This gives potential job applicants an opportunity to ask questions of nurses within the organization. Be sure to get their business cards, as well. Follow-up with an e-mail or hand-written note to keep the connection alive.

Professional Organizations

Membership in professional organizations is another effective way to network with other nurses and learn about opportunities in a variety of settings and practice roles. There are many nursing organizations:

American Nurses Association, Sigma Theta Tau and specialty organizations for experienced nurses and recent graduates. Nursing students can join the National Student Nurses Association, which also includes membership in your state nursing students' organization. If you have the opportunity, take on a committee or leadership position within the association. This will provide positive leadership experience and professional growth, and the activity will look great on your resume.

Gaining Valuable Experience

Susan graduated a year ago with her BSN. The job market in her community is very competitive, and she was unsuccessful in finding an RN position for nearly a year. Unable to relocate because she was recently married, Susan, newly inducted in Sigma Theta Tau, decided to get involved in local chapter activities. She came to Board meetings and volunteered to help with projects. Impressed with her dedication and work ethic, several Board members began looking for openings in their organizations for Susan. When she applied for jobs, they wrote her letters of recommendation and made phone calls on her behalf. Susan soon landed a nursing position. It wasn't her dream job, but she's learning and growing in this role and will have valuable experience to use in future job searches.

Nursing Conferences and Conventions

Attending nursing conferences and conventions is yet another useful networking opportunity. Introduce yourself to some of the nurses and nurse leaders in attendance. Ask them about their organizations. Don't be embarrassed to discuss your qualifications and goals. Be sure to get their business cards and give them yours. Ask if you can contact them regarding openings in their organizations. Follow-up soon after the conference, and remind them where you met. If appropriate, send them your resume. Although there may not currently be job openings suitable for you, ask if you can contact them periodically to check in.

If you invest time in building these relationships, not only will you learn about upcoming job openings, but you'll also begin to build a lasting list of professional contacts, which will be valuable to you— both personally and professionally - throughout your career.

Contacts through Work and School

If you're currently employed as an RN, make contacts with other nurses and managers in the departments that are of interest to you. For example, maybe you're a staff RN who is considering another type of nursing role, such as staff development. Contact the manager or RNs working in the department to learn what qualifications are needed. You may want to visit the department or job shadow to determine whether this role would be a good fit for you.

If you're still in nursing school, but work as a nursing assistant or other role within a health care organization, make it known when you're graduating and that your goal is a staff RN position. If your employment record is positive, you should have an advantage over other applicants.

For those of you who are nursing students, strive to make positive impressions in your clinical rotations. Get to know the nurses. Whenever the opportunity arises, introduce yourself to the department manager. This is especially important during your final semester practicum. Let the people in the department know that you'd like to work there upon graduation.

Using Social Media Sites

Job hunters in today's digital age have the advantage of utilizing social networking to connect with contacts from a wider variety of venues. More and more health care professionals and nursing faculty are joining *Facebook* and other professional networking sites such as *LinkedIn*.

If you don't have a *Facebook* page, then start one. It's easy to do. When you make a contact at a career fair, conference or other event, check to see if the person is on *Facebook*. Send a message reminding them where you met, and request to become a "*Facebook* friend." This is a convenient way to keep in contact with them.

Many health care and community service organizations are also on *Facebook*. You can use these sites to watch for events, opportunities and to learn more about a potential employer.

Before you start using *Facebook* as a networking and job search strategy, peruse your own *Facebook* page. If there are any photos, information or messages you wouldn't want an employer to see, remove them. If you're not on *LinkedIn*, consider joining this site as well. The more you expand your contact list and networking efforts, the more in touch you will be with the people who can help you in your job search.

What __Not__ to Put on *Facebook*

Before you use *Facebook* or other social media sites to network with potential employers and other professional contacts, make sure your page doesn't contain any of the following:

- Derogatory comments
- Party pictures showing alcohol or drugs
- Indecent material or photographs
- Any photos or representation of you that a potential employer would perceive as negative

Try to put yourself in the employer's place and then look critically at your *Facebook* page. Remember, the average nurse manager is over 40 years old. Something you may not initially think is offensive may appear very negative to someone from another generation. If in doubt, remove the photo or post.

Be Respectful of Everyone on Your Journey

Nursing is a service profession. Your customers are your patients and their families, as well as your colleagues, physicians, other staff in the organization and the people in your community. As you look for a job, and throughout your career, treat everyone with respect and courtesy.

I'm sorry to say that I've observed some RN job applicants who exhibit rude behavior to Human Resources staff, unit secretaries and other personnel, and then turn on the charm when meeting the unit manager. One of these applicants actually told me they didn't think it mattered if they were nice to "the other people." Besides the fact that this person was immediately eliminated from all consideration as a potential employee, they're also missing the point of what nursing is all about.

Employers want their staff to personify the mission and values of their organizations at all times, whether on the job or not. And those are the people they strive to hire—every time!

Treat Others with Respect

Kathy, a nursing director in a small community hospital, contacts the Human Resources department before she interviews a potential candidate to find out how they behaved when contacting or visiting the department. If the prospective employee is reported to be rude or disrespectful, Kathy won't interview them. Period! End of story!

The Bottom Line

Whenever possible, network with others. Let them know about your abilities, qualifications and goals. This will help you in your job quest and you'll build valuable relationships that you can nurture throughout your career.

Creating Effective Resumes

"The only real security that you can have in this world is a reserve of knowledge, experience and ability."

Henry Ford

Your resume is a condensed compilation of your qualifications, including education, work experience, professional affiliations, community service and other areas. It's a snapshot view of your skills and abilities. As much as possible, it should reflect you and your style.

The main goal of your resume is to capture the interest of potential employers so you get a job interview. Following the interview, your resume is a reminder of what you have to offer the potential employer.

In this chapter, we'll discuss the major components of your resume and how to best utilize this tool to showcase your qualifications. You'll also learn to develop targeted resumes, tailored to the employment opportunity.

Choose Your Words Carefully

Use high-impact action words, rather than passive words. See the table on page 32 for suggestions. Don't repeat the same words over and over. Use a Thesaurus to find synonyms for key words. Use words strategically. For example—I want to use the word *developed* (I *developed* an education program for diabetes patients). Determine where *developed* will fit best in your resume. Then, when you have the need to repeat the word *developed*, use your Thesaurus to find similar replacement words (created, produced, designed, etc).

Sample Action Words

achieve	graduate	plan
accomplish	increase	prepare
advise	implement	present
analyze	improve	produce
build	innovate	provide
communicate	institute	recommend
compile	instruct	recruit
complete	interpret	reinforce
coordinate	launch	research
create	lecture	revamp
delegate	lead	review
demonstrate	maintain	revise
design	manage	schedule
determine	master	simplify
develop	monitor	solve
direct	motivate	structure
document	negotiate	suggest
establish	operationalize	supervise
expand	orchestrate	support
earn	organize	teach
facilitate	optimize	train
function	oversee	translate
gain	participate	update
generate	perform	write

Key Words

Some employers will scan resumes for "key words" related to the job opening. Resumes that don't contain some of these key words are eliminated from consideration for the position. Look at specific job postings for potential key words the employer is looking for. Be sure to incorporate some of these into your resume.

Resume Length

When searching for a job in a hospital or health care organization, your resume should be 1-2 pages in length. If you're a new grad with limited experience, try to keep the length of your resume at one page. Experienced

RNs may need two pages to capture work experience. Those applying for research or faculty positions usually submit more in-depth resumes, commonly called curriculum vitas (CVs). In addition to material typically found on a resume, CVs also include research projects and teaching experience.

In an effort to limit your resume to one page, don't make the type too small or try to cram too much onto your page. When looking at a document, if a reader encounters too much dark type, not offset by enough white space, the brain tends to ignore or avoid the information. Our eyes and brains are much happier with a balance of blocks of words and white space. Therefore, if your resume is too difficult to read on one page, and you don't want to cut any of the information—use two pages. Creatively use bolding and italics to highlight important areas. For example, make your section headings bold, such as: education, work experience and certifications.

Ideal font size is 12 point. You can reduce to 11 point if necessary, but don't make your typeface any smaller. Remember, the average nurse manager is over 40 years old—a small typeface is more difficult for this age group to read. If the manager has difficulty reading your resume, it's likely to be pushed aside.

Don't pad your resume, thinking that more pages are more impressive. If you add fluff to your resume, then the message about your experience and skills may get lost. Hiring managers are often inundated with large volumes of resumes and applications for open positions. If it's too much work to sift through a resume that's long and cumbersome, chances are it will be thrown in the discard pile.

While some applicants try to pad their resumes, many other job seekers fail to include or showcase key information which sets them apart from other candidates. Let's take a look at important information to include in your resume.

What Should I Include in My Resume?

Your Name and Contact Information
Include street address, e-mail and preferred telephone number. Use a professional email address, such as your name@hotmail.com.

Goal or Objective Statement versus Summary Statement
This statement is a 1-2 sentence declaration at the beginning of your resume that expresses your main goal or objective as a nurse and/or potential employee. Personally, I think this statement takes up space that would be better utilized highlighting your qualifications. However, if you are determined to use an objective or goal statement,

don't say something obvious, such as:

My goal is to obtain a position as a registered nurse on a cardiac unit.

They already know that, because you're applying for a job on their unit. Also, if you apply for another position within the organization, you'll need to change the objective statement to fit the job opening. Now you have multiple resumes floating around the facility with different objectives. They may wonder if you're being sincere about your goals.

If you feel strongly about including a statement at the beginning of your resume, then instead of an objective statement, consider a 1-2 sentence summary of your qualifications.

For example:
New graduate nurse with extensive leadership experience in developing community service programs.

Second career nurse with a strong computer technology skill set to augment my nursing degree.

RN with more than 20 years of patient care experience in a wide variety of acute care and outpatient settings.

Work Experience

- Job title
- Name of company
- Date range for the employment period (March 2010 – Present)
- Brief description of your major job duties—you can use one to three sentences or bullet points.
- Major accomplishments and/or skills learned on the job.
- Optional—include name of supervisor

Generally speaking, list health care related job experience first, then non health care. If separating into two categories, you can name the categories *Health Care Experience* and *Other Work Experience*.

Leadership Experience

Highlight any leadership experience, such as president of the local chapter of the student nurses' association or patient safety rep for your nursing unit. Leadership experience adds another dimension to your skills and shows initiative and commitment.

What Job Experience Should I Include as a New Graduate?

You have little or no health care job experience because you just graduated. Because of this, many of you list all your clinical training courses completed during nursing school. Generally speaking, I don't recommend including this information on your resume. Listing these clinical courses takes up a lot of space and every nursing student in your state will have similar experiences. Instead, focus on your final clinical practicum or externship. As described previously, provide the name of the unit, hospital or organization, dates of the experience and a brief description of your duties.

Please Note—The exception would be if an employer specifically asks you to list the clinical courses you've completed. In that case, always give the potential employer what they ask for. I would create a special resume specifically for that organization (more information about targeting your resume later in this chapter).

Additionally, volunteer activities are valuable experiences you want to capture on your resume. We'll discuss community service/volunteer activities later in this chapter.

Education

List education in chronological order, with the most recent first. Include:

- Name of school
- Degree conferred
- GPA—include only if you recently graduated or you're still in school; don't include if your GPA is less than 3.5
- Month and year you graduated
    - If you didn't graduate from that institution, list years attended
    - Education in progress—indicate anticipated graduation date

Certifications

List any certifications you may have: Basic Life Support, Advanced Cardiac Life Support, chemotherapy certification, arrhythmia interpretation, etc. Also include the date the certification expires. If you have multiple certifications, place under a separate section heading. If you only have one, such as BLS, list it in the Education section.

Community Service

List community service projects or volunteer activities. Include:
- Organization
- Date of service
- Brief description of duties or projects

Awards

List any awards you've received, especially those related to health care and community service.

Professional and Service Organizations

Include organizations you belong to such as National and State Student Nurses Associations, American Nurses Association, Oncology Nurses Society, Emergency Nurses Association, etc. Also list any community and/or service organizations you didn't mention in the Community Service section.

Special Projects

Describe special projects you've completed, either individually or in groups, especially those that are relevant to the position you're applying for. For example, let's say you're an RN working on a telemetry unit. You're applying for a position in your hospital's quality department. Include on your resume any unit projects or initiatives you've been involved in related to improvement of patient care, systems, cost reductions, etc. If you're a nursing student, describe any significant individual or group projects you completed.

Other Accomplishments

Any other experience or accomplishments you haven't listed that you think will make you stand out as a valuable potential employee.

Hobbies

Generally speaking, you shouldn't list hobbies on your resume. However, if you have a hobby that sets you apart from other applicants, put it on your resume. For example, a high level belt in martial arts, such as brown or black, will often set you apart from other applicants. I once worked in a hospital department where the manager hired someone with no prior health care experience mainly because the applicant held a black belt in karate. The manager reasoned that this accomplishment showed drive, determination and a willingness to work hard. He was right—this individual quickly became a stellar member of the team.

Another factor to consider is the amount of information your resume contains. If you have little health care or other experience, then a relevant hobby might balance your resume. However, if you're already having trouble fitting all your qualifications on 1-2 pages, don't list any hobbies.

Tailoring Your Resume to the Needs of the Organization

As discussed in the introduction to this book, the applicant who gets the job is the one who shows that they can best meet the employer's needs. How can you do this? Determine what skills and qualities the employer is looking for. Do you meet those needs? If the answer is yes and you're planning to apply for the job—take a critical look at your resume. Does your resume adequately reflect your qualifications relative to the position? If not, then modify your resume to highlight those qualifications.

For example, I'm an RN with a unique background. Nursing was a second career for me. My first career was in marketing, public relations and writing for publications. I was a cardiac nurse for eight years and have more than 10 years of management and staff development experience. As a result, I have three versions of my resume: one version emphasizes my clinical skills, another highlights my management and staff development experience and the third focuses on my skills in writing and marketing. All versions include my basic qualifications, but each version has a different emphasis. When applying for a job, I start with the version that best meets the needs of my potential employer. I then fine tune that resume to showcase the qualifications I think would be of most interest to the potential employer. This has proven to be a very successful strategy for me.

Let me stress—this is not dishonest! I'm not telling untruths or exaggerating my qualifications. Instead, I'm selecting the most appropriate elements from my list of qualifications to show that I can get the job done. So don't be afraid to adjust, modify and/or tailor your resume for different employers. This is definitely a lot more work, but it will certainly pay off.

Use the tool at the end of this chapter to list all of your qualifications, skills, abilities and attributes. From this list, you can build your basic resume and create other versions, if appropriate. Add to this list as your skills and experience increase. Even if you don't have enough varied experience right now to create multiple versions of your basic resume, you will in the future. This tool can also be useful in drafting your cover letters and preparing for job interviews.

What Employers Look for in Resumes

When examining resumes, potential employers are generally looking for people who:

- Meet the minimum job requirements—including licensure, education, competency.

- Are dependable and consistent—Can the employer count on you? Will you show up for work when scheduled? If you get the job, will you stick with it, even through rough periods?

- Would be a good fit for the department and organization. This includes organizational culture, mission and values.

- Are good communicators. One of the major elements for success as a professional nurse is the ability to communicate with patients, families, physicians and co-workers—often in stressful situations.

- Can work well on a team. Teamwork is essential in health care. Someone who doesn't work well with the team will either quit their job or be disruptive in the workplace.

You may be thinking: How can anyone tell these things just from my resume?

It's true that a resume is just one or two pieces of paper and only provides a brief look at your qualifications. But human resources professionals, recruiters and managers are often very skilled at identifying hints or "red flags" on resumes to help them decide if the candidate is potentially a good employee or one that should be avoided.

Potential red flags on a resume:

- **Does the candidate list many jobs of short duration?** This is a big red flag! An employer doesn't want to invest several months and significant monetary funds and resources to train someone who leaves their position after a short time. Then the employer has to start the process all over again. Frequent job hopping can also indicate that the employee doesn't work well with others or may have been terminated or resigned prior to forced termination. In either case, dependability is an issue.

- **Gaps in employment or education.** The potential employer will often wonder what you've been doing during these gaps. Again, this may indicate undependability or lack of commitment.

- **Multiple errors on resume.** Your resume is your chance to showcase your abilities and sell yourself to potential employers. If your resume contains multiple typos and/or grammatical errors, the employer may question your ability to communicate as well as your attention to detail—both key skills for RNs. Some employers automatically throw out resumes containing multiple errors, regardless of the information in the resume. Using *Spell-Check* isn't enough. Proofread your resume several times. Ask others to review, including peers, nursing faculty, recruiters and others in the nursing profession.

- **There are discrepancies on the resume.** Does one section of your resume contradict another? For example, in one place, you state that you were employed during a certain time period, yet you state other time periods on your job application. This may be a simple mistake, but as noted above, potential employers aren't very tolerant of errors on your resume or application. You should also be aware that there are some job applicants who misrepresent or falsify their qualifications. Discrepancies on a resume and job application may cause an employer to think you're being dishonest about your qualifications. Even if you get the job, misrepresentation can be grounds for dismissal.

Resume Red Flags

- Gaps in work and/or educational history
- Frequent jobs of short duration
- Multiple typos and grammatical errors
- Discrepancies between resume and job application or other documents

You can certainly be sure your resume is free of discrepancies and spelling, typographical and grammatical errors. But what if you have gaps in your resume or a work history where you've changed jobs frequently? You may have a perfectly legitimate reason for these occurrences. How can you convince an employer that you would be a good employee?

Be proactive. Use your cover letter and employment application to explain information on your resume that may be a red flag to a potential employer. We'll discuss this further in our next Chapter: *Your Cover Letter*.

Uploading Your Resume for Online Job Applications

Most online job sites give you the option to upload your resume as part of your job application. Always include your resume if you have the option to do so. Many sites require you to enter some of the information from your resume, such as employment history and educational institutions, along with contact information. Having a paper copy of your resume when completing these online applications will expedite the process.

Some sites require you to cut and paste your resume onto the site, which may strip your formatting. Develop a basic version of your resume that doesn't contain bolding, italics and other special formatting. Use this version for cutting and pasting onto non html-friendly job sites. After a cut and paste, always review the material to make sure none of your text shifted or was deleted.

Frequently Asked Questions About Resumes

I won't graduate from nursing school for another year. I've tried to get a job as a nursing assistant, but there are no openings in the hospitals in my community. What can I do to get some health care experience?

If there are no openings for nursing assistants, look for other health care positions such as patient transportation, unit assistant or even food service. This may not be exactly what you were looking for, but will get your foot in the door. If paid positions aren't available or practical, look for volunteer opportunities in health care settings, community health and/or community service organizations.

In addition, check with your nursing faculty and/or the manager of the unit where you currently have your clinical rotation about arranging a special project you can complete within the department. Perhaps you can earn extra credit or units for this endeavor. This provides good experience, and may get the department manager's attention.

Also consider joining a mission trip to an underserved area during school vacations. All these experiences contribute to your professional growth and are impressive on your resume.

Nursing is a second career for me. Do I include my experience from my previous career?

Yes, absolutely! Many managers love to hire second degree RNs. Because of their previous experience and skills, they often add another dimension to the nursing team. For example, a previous career in a high tech field such as computer science would be an asset. With all the new developments in health information technology, an employee with a computer technology background can play a key role in training and utilization on the unit.

You may not have room on your resume to list every job you've held during your previous career, but you can certainly list the types of jobs and highlight major experience. Select the experience and skills you think will be of interest to health care employers. Also be ready to discuss your prior skills during the job interview.

Do I include references on my resume?

Usually include only if the employer asks for them with the resume. Most employers don't ask for references until they've narrowed the field to a few top candidates. If you're currently employed and your boss doesn't know you're looking for another job, you don't want the potential employer calling for a reference before you've spoken to your supervisor. So, if you include your boss as a reference, make sure they are aware of it before calls are made.

Space on the resume is limited and valuable. In most cases, you don't have room to include references. The exception is if your resume is 1½ pages, you may want to use the remaining space to list references. Also, if you have a reference you think might have some clout with your potential employer—you'll want to include that reference.

The Bottom Line

Use your resume to showcase your skills, abilities and talents. Emphasize the qualifications that will best meet the employer's needs and help you stand out from the crowd.

Assessment Tool #2 - **My Qualifications**

Use the worksheets on the following pages to compile and describe your skills, talents, attributes, education, experience, credentials and personal characteristics. You can then use these worksheets to build your resume, write your cover letter, complete job applications and assist you in preparing for job interviews.

Add to this tool as your experience and qualifications grow. It will be a useful resource for you.

My Qualities and Personal Attributes
For example: compassionate, creative, analytical, loyal, honest, etc.

Special Skills and Abilities
Such as: bilingual, expertise with computers, good communicator, leadership skills, etc.

Leadership Experience
Including: supervisory experience, charge nurse, team leader, officer in a professional organization, student leader, etc.

Work Experience

Job #1 *(for new grads, could be your final semester practicum or externship)*

Job Title:

Dates of Employment or Experience:

Employer:

Supervisor:

City, State:

Major Duties:

Accomplishments:

Special Projects:

Skills you learned or developed:

Job #2

Job Title:

Dates of Employment or Experience:

Employer:

Supervisor:

City, State:

Major Duties:

Accomplishments:

Special Projects:

Skills you learned or developed:

Job #3

Job Title:

Dates of Employment or Experience:

Employer:

Supervisor:

City, State:

Major Duties:

Accomplishments:

Special Projects:

Skills you learned or developed:

Education

School #1

Educational Institution:

City, State:

Degree (or expected degree):

Major or area of study:

Date degree conferred, expected graduation date, or years of attendance:

School #2

Educational Institution:

City, State:

Degree (or expected degree):

Major or area of study:

Date degree conferred, expected graduation date, or years of attendance:

School #3

Educational Institution:

City, State:

Degree (or expected degree):

Major or area of study:

Date degree conferred, expected graduation date, or years of attendance:

Certifications

Certification #1

Name or type of certification:

Organization or agency:

Expiration date or date issued:

Certification #2

Name or type of certification:

Organization or agency:

Expiration date or date issued:

Awards and Honors

Award #1

Name of Award/Honor:

Organization:

Date:

Award #2

Name of Award/Honor

Organization:

Date:

Community Service

Organization/Project #1

Name of Organization:

Date of Service:

Project or Major Duties:

Organization/Project #2

Name of Organization:

Date of Service:

Project or Major Duties:

Organization/Project #3

Name of Organization:

Date of Service:

Project or Major Duties:

Professional and Service Organizations

Organization #1

Name of Organization:

Offices Held (if applicable):

Activities:

Dates:

Organization #2

Name of Organization:

Offices Held (if applicable):

Activities:

Dates:

Organization #3

Name of Organization:

Offices Held (if applicable):

Activities:

Dates:

Special Projects

Describe any major special projects you completed on the job or as a student, including individual and group projects.

Project #1

Name of Project:

Description:

Project Time Period:

Individual or Group:

Project #2

Name of Project:

Description:

Project Time Period:

Individual or Group:

Project #3

Name of Project:

Description:

Project Time Period:

Individual or Group:

Other Accomplishments

Use this space to list any other relevant experience, projects or accomplishments you haven't previously listed, such as publishing an article, teaching an inservice, mentoring a colleague or peer, etc.

Hobbies

List and describe any relevant hobbies. You probably won't list hobbies on your resume, but this may provide some information or anecdotes you could use in job interviews or informal conversations with professional contacts or potential employers.

Sample Resumes

Experienced RN Resume

Andrew S. Wilson, BSN, RN
5200 First Street
Sherman Oaks, CA 91423
Cell: (818) 777-8888 ♦ Home: (818) 444-9999 ♦ andrewwilson@email.com

Experience

Big City University Hospital
Burbank, California

Staff Nurse, Oncology Unit
July 2007 – Present

I provide total care for oncology patients on a 28 bed unit, including: medication and chemotherapy administration, pain control, symptom management, support for terminally ill patients and patient and family education. I am frequently charge nurse, responsible for 5-8 RNs, 2 nursing assistants and other support personnel. I am also a preceptor for RNs newly hired to our unit.

Staff Nurse, Surgical Unit
June 2003 – June 2007

As a staff RN on this fast-paced unit, I delivered primary nursing care for pre- and post-operative surgical patients. Nursing responsibilities included: IV therapy, administration of blood products, wound care, pain management, monitoring of vital signs and post-op and discharge teaching for patients and families.

Good Shepard Hospital
San Diego, California

Nurse Technician, Float Pool
January 2002 – May 2003

As a member of the hospital float pool, I performed a wide range of duties under RN supervision. During my tenure, I worked several shifts in every unit of the hospital.

Education

Bachelor of Science in Nursing, University of California, Los Angeles. May 2010

Associate Degree in Nursing—Saddleback College, Mission Viejo, California. May 2003

Special Projects and Accomplishments

Stand Up to Cancer Retreat—May 1, 2010. Hospital-sponsored event for cancer patients and their families. I was a member of the planning team and a session facilitator.

Medication Administration Observer—January 2010 – present.
I observe RN medication administration procedures and gather data to submit to the Collaborative Alliance for Nursing Outcomes. Goal is to reduce medication errors.

Organizations

Sigma Theta Tau International, Nursing Honor Society, Inducted May 2010.

American Nurses Association, June 2003 – present

Oncology Nursing Society, January 2008 - present

Certifications

Oncology Certified Nurse, expires June 2012

Basic Cardiac Life Support, expires September 2011

References Available Upon Request

New RN Graduate Resume

Elizabeth Brown, BSN, RN

123 A Street, Sacramento, CA, 95819
Home phone: 916-456-1234; Cell phone: 916-222-3333; E-mail: ebrown@xxxx.com

Health Care Experience

Surgical Unit, City Community Hospital, Santa Rosa, California
Final Semester Practicum: January – May, 2010

- Under the supervision of an RN, provided bedside patient care for 3-4 patients on the day shift.
- Responsibilities included: assessment, medication administration, dressing changes, IV care and maintenance, post-op recovery and other nursing care.
- Clinical documentation on electronic medical record.
- Educated patients regarding wound management, home care, discharge and other topics.

Sonoma County Vaccination Clinic
September 2009

- Under the supervision of an RN, vaccinated adults and children at three migrant worker camps.

Counselor for *Summer-Fun*, a Camp for Disabled Children; Echo Lake, California
July – August, 2009

- Provided education, supervision and recreation activities for disabled children, ages 10 – 13.

Other Employment Experience

Meredith's Café, Rohnert Park, California
June 2008 – May 2010

- Server for restaurant with 20 tables. Duties include: customer service, ensuring patron orders are accurate and operating cash register.

California State Fair, Sacramento
August 2006 and 2007

- Counter server at food concession stand.

Accomplishments

Dean's Honor Roll

- Sonoma State University: Fall 2009; Spring 2010

Dragon Fire Martial Arts

- Achieved the rank of Black Belt
- Taught sections of classes and entire classes (2004 – 2009)

Education

Sonoma State University: Bachelor of Science in Nursing; May 2010

American River College, Sacramento: general education courses; January 2006 – May 2008

Organizations and Community Service Activities

California Nursing Students' Association

- 2009-2010 Sonoma State Chapter Treasurer

Loaves and Fishes Homeless Shelter and Kitchen, Sacramento, California

- Prepared meals and provided counter service for homeless and needy clients.

References Available Upon Request

Second Career as an RN Resume

KARLA LOPEZ-JOHNSON, RN
600 Anywhere Blvd.
Fresno, CA 93650
Cell: (559) 345-9292; Home: (559) 543-8822
Klopezjohnson@myemail.com

Newly licensed second career RN with proven communication and leadership skills.

Bilingual: English and Spanish

Health Care Experience

ABC Community Hospital – Cardiac Telemetry Unit
Final Semester Externship: January – May, 2010
- Provided bedside patient care for up to four patients under the supervision of an RN preceptor.
- Responsibilities included: assessment, medication administration, respiratory treatments, post-procedure recovery, arrhythmia interpretation and other nursing care.
- Educated patients and families about disease management, medications, discharge and other topics.
- Observed cardiac surgery, cardiac catheterization and pacemaker placement.

Fresno County Health Fair/Screening
February 2010
- Measured blood pressures, height and weight. Discussed risk factors and heart healthy living. Translated information for Spanish-speaking participants

Volunteer, Fresno School District
September – December, 2009
- Assisted school nurse in conducting student health assessments, including weight, height and blood pressure measurement, and vision testing.

Other Employment Experience

Director of Public Relations
California Association of Rehabilitation Facilities
April 2004 – July 2007

- Communicated with the media and association membership regarding important issues related to rehabilitation for the developmentally disabled.
- Created and maintained the organization's website and produced newsletters and other publications.

Staff Writer
Pacific Public Relations and Advertising
June 2000 – March 2004

- Wrote press releases, advertisements and radio spots.
- Collaborated with creative team to design advertising campaigns for numerous clients.

Coordinator of Internal Communications
ABC Manufacturing
June 1998 – May 2000

- Produced internal newsletters and other publications for the company's 900 employees.

(Continued)

Lopez-Johnson Resume
Page 2

Recent Leadership Experience

California Nursing Students' Association Chapter
Fresno City College
2009 – 2010 President
2008 – 2009 Vice President

Education

Fresno City College: Associate Degree in Nursing; May 2010

Oregon State University: Bachelor of Science in Communications Studies; May 2000

Lane Community College, Eugene Oregon: general education; September 1996 – May 1998

Certifications

Advanced Cardiac Life Support; expires May 2012

Basic Cardiac Monitoring Certification, completed April 2010; no expiration

Basic Cardiac Life Support; expires May 2012

Organizations and Community Service Activities

American Nurses Association
June 2010 – present

Association of California Nurse Leaders
June 2010 - present

California Nursing Students' Association
September 2008 – May 2010

Girl Scouts, Troop 675
September 2008 - present
Leader for a troop of 12 girls, ages 10 – 12

References Available Upon Request

Your Cover Letter 5

"Things may come to those who wait, but only the things left by those who hustle."

Abraham Lincoln

Your cover letter is your introduction to your potential employer. It's a brief, but critically important way to present yourself and let the employer know you're interested specifically in their job opening.

A few years ago, nurses applied for jobs by submitting a paper application and resume. Usually accompanying the resume was a cover letter. Today, the vast majority of job contenders apply for positions online. But that doesn't mean a well-written cover letter is any less important. Most online applications give you an opportunity to include a message. This is the modern version of the cover letter.

Think of your cover letter as an infomercial for yourself. A vehicle to highlight and showcase your key attributes. Use it to connect your abilities and expertise with the requirements of the job and the needs of the employer.

Sample Letter - New Graduate

To Whom It May Concern:

I was delighted to discover on your website that you have three open positions for new graduate registered nurses on your Medical/Surgical unit. I believe I possess the qualities that will make me a valuable asset to your patient care team.

I recently graduated from (nursing school). During my final semester externship, I spent eight weeks on the fast-paced Med/Surg unit at ABC Healthcare. By the end of my clinical rotation, I was effectively managing four patients. My duties included: physical assessment, medication administration, blood products administration, recovery of post-op patients, patient education, assisting with procedures and charting using the electronic medical record.

In addition, I was treasurer of our school's chapter of the California Nursing Students' Association. As treasurer, I was responsible for managing chapter funds, paying bills and preparing monthly reports for Board and Chapter meetings.

Please review my resume included with this application. I would very much appreciate the opportunity to discuss my qualifications relative to the needs of your Med/Surg unit. Feel free to contact me if I can provide any further information.

I look forward to hearing from you.

Sample Letter - Experienced RN

Dear Hiring Manager:

I read with interest the job description for the registered nurse position in your Family Birth Center. Women's health is my passion. As an RN, I have more than ten years experience in patient care, with the last six being in labor and delivery and ante-partum units at EFG Medical Center.

In addition to my patient care experience, I am certified in childbirth education and lactation counseling and have taught classes in both areas for three years. I have also participated in several quality improvement projects within my units.

Educationally, I have a BSN from (nursing school) and have recently begun the MSN program in nursing administration at (nursing school).

Thank you for considering me for a position in your Family Birth Center. I look forward to discussing my qualifications relative to this position at your earliest convenience.

Explaining Gaps in Your Resume

The cover letter is also a vehicle to explain any information on your resume that might appear negative to potential employers. In the previous chapter, *Creating Effective Resumes*, we discussed that some work histories may be viewed negatively by hiring managers.

These include: short job tenure, frequent job changes and/or large gaps in employment and/or education history. The cover letter gives you a valuable opportunity to explain these potential red flags. Utilize it.

For example:

"As you can see by my resume, there is a two year gap in my job experience between 2006 and 2008. During this time, I left my job to care for my mother, who was terminally ill. Caring for her on a daily basis made me realize that nursing was the career for me. I enrolled in my local community college, completed my prerequisite courses and entered nursing school. Now that I have graduated, I look forward to beginning my career as a nurse."

OR:

"As you can see by my resume, I have held multiple positions of short duration over the past two years. Normally, I am not an employee who moves from job to job, but in this case it was unavoidable. Due to the economy, MNO Home Health closed its doors. Later, I was laid off as a result of massive reductions in staff at QRS Health Care."

Your cover letter also provides the hiring manager with another example of your writing and communication skills. As with your resume, it's critical that your cover letter is free of spelling, grammatical and typographical errors. So before you hit the *Enter* or *Send* button, make sure you proofread your cover letter/message. Better yet—type it, proofread it at least twice, then cut and paste the message into the employer's website. Proofread it again to ensure that nothing was accidentally deleted or jumbled when pasted into the website.

Make sure your cover letter is short, concise and highlights key qualifications. Don't rehash your entire resume. And, whenever possible, connect your qualifications with the specifics of the job opening.

The Bottom Line

Your cover letter/message is an effective tool to highlight your key qualifications and talents. It can also be used to explain any gaps or red flags on your resume.

Preparing for Your Job Interview

"A prudent person foresees the difficulties ahead and prepares for them; the simpleton goes blindly on and suffers the consequences."

Book of Proverbs

You submitted your online application to the health care organization that appears to be a good fit for your skills, abilities and values. You included a resume and message (cover letter) targeted to the requirements of the open position and needs of the employer. Your efforts have paid off—they want to interview you!

Now the hard work begins again...

How can you best communicate your skills, experience and values?

How can you best demonstrate your unique qualifications during the interview?

The key to success on the job interview is: preparation... preparation...and more preparation!

The candidates who get the jobs are the ones who provide thorough and thoughtful answers to the questions presented. These are the applicants who prove they will best meet the employer's needs. This doesn't happen accidentally. It's a function of preparation and planning. This chapter will help you prepare for your upcoming job interview.

What Employers are Looking for During a Job Interview

In order to get ready for the interview, you should have a general understanding of what employers are looking for. We discussed this topic in Chapter 2, *What Employers Are Looking For* and Chapter 3, *Creating Effective Resumes*. If needed, review these chapters again to gain a clear understanding of the general characteristics hiring managers are seeking in potential employees.

In general, most potential employers are looking for:
- clinical competence
- professionalism
- good communication skills
- collaborative team skills
- customer/patient focus
- personal commitment and values aligned with the organization's mission

Job Interview Strategies: Doing Your Homework

Learn all you can about the organization—continue the research you began when applying for the position.

- Visit the organization's website.

- Talk to people who work there—ideally someone from the department with the open position. What types of patients do they see most frequently? What are the benefits of working there? What are the challenges?

- If you haven't already had a tour of the hospital, ask the recruiter for one. Be sure the tour includes the department considering you for a position. Tell the recruiter you have a job interview scheduled. If the recruiter can't give you a guided tour in time for your interview, then explore the hospital as a visitor. Get a feel for the place. If possible, walk through the unit with the job opening (you won't be able to visit some areas, including intensive care units and the emergency department). Does the department seem efficient and organized, or stressed and chaotic? How does the staff interact with patients? Visitors? Each other? You can learn valuable information by simply observing. Sometimes independent observation will give you more insight than a guided tour.

- Check the organization's scores on websites that rank hospitals and their services. This will give you a glimpse into the strengths of the facility as well as areas for improvement.

- Find out who will be interviewing you. When someone calls you to set up the meeting, it's acceptable to ask who will be conducting the interview. Is it the department manager? Is it a panel interview? Once you know the interviewer's name, you can search the organizational website or even utilize *Google* or another search engine to learn more about them. You may learn some valuable information to help you better connect with the interviewer during your meeting.

Researching the organization provides you with information and insights you can interject during the interview. This simple act sends many positive messages to the interviewer: you're thorough and well prepared; you're willing to go the extra mile to achieve your goals; and you're interested enough in the organization to learn more about it.

Sharpen Your Clinical Knowledge

What type of nursing department are you hoping to join? Neurology? Pediatrics? Women's health? Whatever the area, review basic pathophysiology and nursing care for the types of patients predominately seen on the unit. This holds true whether you're a new grad or an experienced nurse seeking to switch to a new area of practice. To gauge your clinical competency for the unit, you will almost certainly be asked some questions regarding the care of these types of patients.

Also, think about patients you've cared for in this same area of specialty. You may be able to utilize some of these examples during the interview to further demonstrate your knowledge and competency.

If you're an RN with past experience in the general area of focus, find out what the specific focus of the unit is. For example, cardiac care is a very wide field. You may have experience on a medical telemetry unit, but the position you're seeking is on an interventional cardiology unit. Don't assume that your past experience will carry you. Learn more about interventional cardiology so that you can relevantly discuss specific patient care needs during the interview.

No Interview is a Sure Thing!

Maybe you performed your nursing school externship on the unit; perhaps you're a nurse on a nearby unit and you've floated to this department before; or possibly you're already an employee, simply applying for a different position. Even so—no interview is a sure thing! Advanced preparation is critical to your success.

Steve was a department supervisor who assumed the manager role on an interim basis when the current manager resigned. He held the role for several months and did well running the day-to-day operations of the department.

When the job position was finally posted, Steve applied for the job. I offered to help him with interview practice, but he felt it wasn't necessary. After all, he had been performing the job successfully for several months. Although I urged Steve to reconsider, he went through the interview process with minimal preparation. During a tough panel interview, he was confronted with questions he had not considered, and did not perform well. In the end, someone else was hired for the job.

Truthfully, Steve was the best candidate for the position, but he didn't prove it during the interview. And because there were people on the interview panel who didn't know him, Steve was not selected for the position.

There is no substitute for preparation...It is the key to success on your job interview!

Anticipate Questions You will be Asked

Now that you've researched the organization, you can build a list of potential interview questions.

To do that, let's review what we've learned so far. We know that most employers are looking for professionally and clinically competent nurses who are dependable, have good communication skills, work effectively in teams, focus on the needs of the patient/customer and are aligned with the vision and values of their organization. Add to this the specific information you learned about the organization through your research.

Now, put yourself in the interviewer's place. What questions would you ask to determine these skills and qualifications in potential job applicants? This is how experienced interviewers select their questions. In many organizations, Human Resources departments often have question banks with a wide range of potential interview questions to choose from. Interviewers pick the questions that will help them best identify the candidates they want to hire.

There are several types of interview techniques and questions. Most interviewers use a combination of these methods and corresponding questions.

Interview Questions and Techniques

Learning More About You

The interviewer wants to know how you see yourself, and is trying to gain insight into your personality and motivations. Some of the common questions in this category are:

- *Tell me about yourself*—many interviews start with this general question. It sets the context for the interview. I highly recommend that you prepare and practice a 1½ - 3 minute description of yourself to answer this question. Focus on the highlights of your job experience and education. This description will also come in handy if you find yourself in impromptu conversations with potential employers at conferences, job fairs or in other situations.

  Leave out personal information! *Tell me about yourself* is the first question I've asked every job applicant I've ever interviewed. I can't tell you how many times I've heard about an applicant's parents, their siblings, their dog or Uncle Fred. This is useless information and tells me that this candidate is not well prepared to discuss their qualifications. As a general rule, the only personal information that is relevant is why you became a nurse. For example: "After taking care of my grandmother for two years, I wanted to make caring for people my life's work."

- *Where do you see yourself in 2 years, 5 years, 10 years; or, what are your short and long term career goals?* Interviewers often want to know about your plans for the future. Think about where you see yourself in relation to the job opening and the hiring organization.

  If you're a new grad, you may not know what your long term goals are yet. It's okay to say this—if you include an explanation. For example: "My short term goal is to get my nursing career off to a good start by hardwiring my skills, expanding my clinical knowledge and learning my role as an RN. Once I feel more comfortable as a nurse, I will be able to set meaningful future goals."

- *What are your strengths and weaknesses?* This is a favorite interview question that has been around for years. Personally, I don't like it or use it, but many others do—so be prepared. Name your top 1-2 strengths and quickly elaborate on how they relate to your ability to excel in this job: "I'm very organized, which enables me to manage a large patient load, even on a busy day."

   Also, be ready to describe a weakness. Many candidates who are unprepared for this question, panic and say: "I don't have any weaknesses." No interviewer is going to buy that one! Be prepared. Focus on a weakness and how you've dealt with it and turned it into a positive: "I'm an over-achiever and often set high standards for myself and others. This sometimes results in frustration. I've learned to be more realistic in setting goals for myself and recognize that I must let others set their own goals."

Behavioral Interviewing

This is currently the fastest growing and most popular interview technique. The basic premise of behavioral interviewing is that past performance is the best indicator of future performance. Utilizing behavioral questions, the interviewer will ask you to describe a situation and your role in it, related to a specific topic.
Some examples are:
- Describe a communication problem you had with someone and how you resolved it.
- Tell me about a time when you dealt with a difficult patient, family member or customer. What happened? How did you resolve the situation?

Behavioral techniques are a key component of most interviews. We will thoroughly explore behavioral interviewing and preparing for behavioral questions in the next chapter.

Situational Interviewing

The interviewer provides you with a scenario, and you explain how you would solve the problem or resolve the situation.
For example:

- Sally, the night shift nurse who often takes over your patient load is frequently late for work, and no one else seems to be doing anything about it. What would you do?

Once very popular in the health care setting, many interviewers have replaced situational questions with behavioral ones. One of the problems with situational questions is that many job candidates know how they *should* react in certain situations. But instead, the interviewer wants to determine how they *will* act. Behavioral interviewing questions are a more reliable indicator of behavior than situational questions.

You may be asked some situational interview questions related to clinical issues, such as:
You've determined that your new admit, a 72 year-old woman with pneumonia and confusion, is a fall risk. What steps would you take to keep her safe from falling?

Another popular situational question is related to prioritization:
It's a busy morning on your unit. Here's what's happening:

a. Your post-op patient is asking for pain medication
b. Your newly admitted patient is complaining of chest pain
c. A family member wants to speak to you
d. You're notified by the lab of a critical value
e. An MD is on the telephone and wants to give routine orders for a patient

What would you do?

Obviously, you can't be in five places at once. The key to this question is prioritization and delegation. Different RNs may answer it a little differently, but the interviewer wants to know that you'll handle the most critical concern first—the patient complaining of chest pain. Another key element is asking others for help. Explain how you would prioritize and delegate.

If you're an experienced RN, you may have dealt with similar situations before. After explaining how you would handle this particular situation, you can dazzle the interviewer by providing a specific example of how you prioritize and delegate in your nursing practice.

See pages 76-80 for more sample interview questions.

Practice Your Answers

Once you've created a list of potential interview questions, develop your answers. Practice with a friend or in front of a mirror. Take note of your body language and facial expressions. Nonverbal messages are very important. Studies have shown that when nonverbal and verbal messages are conflicting, people are more likely to believe the nonverbal message. So, make sure your body language and facial expressions complement your verbal message.

Be Aware of Your Nonverbal Messages

Practice in front of a mirror to increase your awareness of your body language. In some cases, people are unaware that their facial expressions, gestures or body language send a negative message. For example, when you are deep in thought, perhaps you frown? You may be unaware of this, but in an interview situation, the hiring manager may interpret your frown as anger or unhappiness. These negative messages may cost you the job!

A survey of 2,500 employers, conducted by CareerBuilder, found that a job candidate's body language during the interview greatly affects hiring decisions. More than two-thirds of those surveyed said that failure to make eye contact could cost the applicant their chance at the job. More than a third said that failure to smile negatively impacts the interview. And, a third of the respondents said that poor posture would hurt the job seeker's chances.

Through awareness of your body language, you can train yourself to ensure that your nonverbal messages reinforce your verbal ones.

As you prepare for an upcoming job interview, practice in front of a mirror to increase your awareness of your body language and facial expressions. Many interviewers respond positively to smiles and negatively when a job candidates frowns. Make sure your body language and facial expressions match the message you are delivering.

Focus on the Employer's Needs

Remember, the successful job candidate will be the one the employer determines is the best fit for the job. If you focus on the employer's needs and how you can meet those needs—your chances for success skyrocket.

The Bottom Line

Preparation and practice are the keys to success in job interviews. Make a list of potential interview questions, and practice your answers with friends and colleagues who are willing to help you. Practicing in front of a mirror is another strategy to increase your awareness of body language and facial expressions.

Behavioral Interviewing Techniques

"Words tell...but stories sell!"

Popular Advertising and Sales Adage

Behavioral interviewing has grown in popularity in recent years, and is a technique used in some form by many potential employers. Instead of asking questions about hypothetical scenarios, the interviewer asks the job seeker to provide an example of how they handled a certain type of situation in the past. For example: "Tell me about an emergency patient situation you were involved in and how you handled it."

The basic premise of behavioral interviewing is that past behavior is the best indicator of future behavior. In scenario-based questions, most job applicants know how they *should* react and can describe hypothetical actions. However, what an employer wants to know is how you *would* act in a given situation. Your past behavior in a situation is the best indicator of your future actions in similar circumstances.

Question Structure

Behavioral interview questions are open-ended to obtain complete information, rather than simple yes or no answers. The interviewer strives to avoid "textbook answers," and instead is trying to learn how you responded under certain circumstances. Behavioral information provides the potential employer with factual evidence of what the job candidate has done—or failed to do—in a given situation.

Generally, behavioral interviewing questions are composed of three areas:

1) Lead question—asks for your behavior in a certain circumstance. The interviewer is looking for actual experiences and resulting behaviors. Lead questions usually begin with: *tell me about a time...describe a situation when...give me an example of...*

2) Probing questions—can be asked to garner more information about the situation, actions or outcomes. Probing questions often ask for who, what, where, how, why. For example: What specific steps did you take? How did you complete the project? Why was that important? What did you say to the complaining patient? Probing questions can be an indicator that you're not providing thorough enough examples that completely explain the situation, action and outcomes. As you answer other behavioral questions during the interview, try to provide more complete answers, especially when describing your actions.

3) Summary question—may be used to clarify or check for understanding. The interviewer will briefly summarize all or part of your answer and ask you if their interpretation of events is accurate. If any key points are left out or not correct, clarify for the interviewer.

Past Behavior is the Best Indicator of Future Behavior

An operating room manager attending a seminar I was conducting on behavioral interview techniques related this story: I was interviewing candidates for an RN vacancy in my OR. One nurse had a long list of experience, but she had left her past two jobs after less than six months. When I asked her why, she explained that the surgical teams in both these organizations were difficult to get along with and there was too much conflict. I knew I had a great surgical team that worked well together, so I believed her previous problems wouldn't be an issue. As a result, I hired her. Now four months later, there are multiple conflicts on my OR team—and she's the root cause of most of them. Her past job history should have been a red flag to me. I should have at least questioned her more thoroughly about her communication/conflict resolution skills, which seem to be totally lacking. Her disruptive behavior far outweighs her strong clinical skills.

More and more managers are realizing that past behavior can be a powerful indicator of future behavior.

Preparing for Behavioral Interviewing Questions

To best prepare for behavioral interview questions, first look at the sample questions at the end of this chapter. Think about how you can best answer those questions by utilizing events and stories from your past. Some stories will come very easily and quickly to you. Others may require more thought as you sift through your past experiences. Whenever possible, utilize stories from your clinical experience.

If you have multiple stories to tell, and are trying to decide which is best, use this *story-telling hierarchy*:

1. Examples from clinical situations or your health care work experience

2. Stories from nursing school (for new grads or those in advanced degree programs)

3. Past employment

4. Other schooling

5. Teams or organizations

6. Friends and family

Once you've identified an example or event from your past, practice telling and re-telling it a few times. When telling the story, don't ramble on. Relay the example completely, yet concisely. You want to provide a complete picture of how you approached a certain situation. Determine the key points, and make sure they come across. When telling your story, be sure to emphasize:

- **Situation**—what happened? What were the circumstances?
- **Action**—how did you respond to the situation?
- **Outcome**—what was the result or impact of your actions?

The action is the key information in the story because it tells the interviewers what you said or did in response to the situation. Actions might include:

- The steps you took to complete a task or project
- The planning process you utilized to:
    - Care for a complicated patient
    - Complete a work assignment
    - Discuss a difficult subject with your supervisor or teacher
- How you handled a conflict situation with a patient, co-worker or fellow student

Obviously, you would like to describe situations in which your actions had profoundly positive outcomes. But, what if the outcome of your story isn't as positive as you'd like it to be?

Choose a different story that more positively illustrates what the interviewer is looking for. If you can only think of the one example that didn't have a great outcome, be sure to tell the interviewer what you learned from the experience and what you'd do differently in the future if confronted with a similar situation.

Sometimes interviewers will ask for negative examples, such as: *Tell me about a time when you had a conflict with another person that didn't go so well?* As described above, after you've told the story, identify what you learned from this experience and how you would behave differently in the future. If you learned something from the experience that you were able to apply in another situation—all the better! Be ready to briefly relay this to the interviewer.

Remember—no one is perfect! The interviewer is trying to get a clear picture of who you are and how you handle situations you may be confronted with in the job. No one expects total perfection; and frankly, the interviewer will probably be skeptical if you try to convince them you've perfectly and expertly handled every situation that has challenged you.

What if you can't think of an example to answer the question? You will probably be asked questions about generic topics, including communication skills, conflict resolution and patient/customer service. If you can't think of an example that occurred in health care, then look outside of health care (*See story-telling hierarchy on page 73*). If you need some time to think, it's perfectly acceptable to ask for a moment to consider your answer. Good interviewers will allow you time to pause and think before responding. If you absolutely cannot come up with a specific example from your past, then tell the interviewer how you would handle a hypothetical situation.

Practicing your answers before the interview doesn't mean you must memorize every possible question and answer. This is impossible. Instead, have a mental outline and idea of how you would answer potential questions. Look for ways to improve and consolidate your answers. This will help you build confidence and increase your comfort level. And as all nurses know—practicing a skill increases your ability to perform the skill better each time.

Practice by Thinking of Your Own Behavioral Questions

Although this book contains many examples of interview questions, this is certainly not a complete list. Think of questions you would ask as an interviewer, and add them to the list.

As you're preparing for job interviews, look at the categories of questions, including team work, communications, clinical competence, etc. What situations or stories can you tell, related to these categories? If you have those situations in mind, then during the interview you are more likely to be able to adapt them to a specific question. For instance, an example you may have practiced involving your communication skills when caring for a difficult patient may be the perfect answer for a question related to customer service. Be flexible so that you can apply your examples to other questions if need be.

The Bottom Line

Prepare! Prepare! Prepare! This will build your confidence and increase your chances for success during the interview.

Sample Interview Questions

General Questions

Tell me about yourself...
(This is your 1 - 3 minute infomercial about yourself)

Describe your education, training and work experiences that will help you be successful in this position.

Why did you apply for this job?

Why do you want to work for this organization?

Why do you think you're the right person for the job?

What is your greatest strength?

What is your greatest area of weakness?

Why did you leave your last job, or why do you want to leave your present position?
(Never speak negatively about a current or former employer!)

Patient Care/Clinical Questions

It's a very busy morning on the unit. Here's what happening...

- Post-op patient is asking for pain med
- Patient c/o chest pain
- A family member wants to speak to you
- You're notified by the lab of a critical value
- MD is on telephone and wants to give routine orders for a patient

How do you handle this? What do you do first?

You've determined that your 80 y/o female patient, with a diagnosis of colon cancer, is at high risk for falls. What steps would you take to keep her safe?

Hospital-acquired infections pose a significant risk to patients on our unit. Describe some general strategies to reduce the risk of hospital acquired infections.

Your patient has a Foley catheter. What is the minimum amount of urine the patient should excrete during your eight hour shift? The Foley bag only contains half that amount, and the bag has not been emptied all shift. What are possible causes? What should you do?

The majority of patients on our nursing unit are elderly with limited mobility. These patients are at increased risk for pressure ulcers. When caring for these patients, what interventions would you utilize to reduce the risk of hospital-acquired pressure ulcers?

Competence in Specific Clinical Areas

Be prepared for some questions to measure your competency in the clinical area you're applying for. The following questions are samples to give you an idea of patient care questions you may be asked. Actual questions will vary depending on the type of unit where you are seeking employment (neurology, oncology, post partum, pediatrics, etc). Before your interview, review the pathophysiology and basic care for these patients.

Your 71 y/o male post-op patient is complaining of a severe headache. When he tries to lift a glass of water with his left hand, it falls from his grasp. When you look at his face, the right side of his mouth looks droopy. What do you think is going on? What should you do?

Mrs. Smith is a 68 y/o patient being evaluated for new onset of chest pain/rule out myocardial infarction. You are about to begin her assessment. What questions would you ask her and what data do you need to know?

On the post-partum unit, you've just been assigned a 32 year-old patient who delivered an 8 lb 8 oz. girl two hours prior. What type of assessment would you make and what key data would you collect for this patient?

Behavioral Interview Questions

Communication Skills/Conflict Resolution

Tell me about a time you had a conflict with another person. What happened? What did you do?

Describe a time when you had a conflict with another person that did not have a positive outcome. What if anything, would you do differently?

Tell me about a time when you and another person had difficulty communicating with each other.

Describe a time when you had to work with a difficult person— could be a patient, customer, supervisor, co-worker, student or professor.

Customer Service/Patient-Family Centered

Describe a time when you interacted with a patient or family member who had difficulty understanding you or complying with your instructions.

Tell me about a situation when a patient or customer needed special care or attention. What did you do?

Describe a time when you had to work with multiple patients/ customers in a high-stress situation with multiple demands. How did you meet all your patient/customer's needs?

Teamwork

Describe a situation when you helped a co-worker who appeared to have difficulty completing an assignment.

Tell me about a time when you had to work with one or more people to complete a task or project.

Describe a situation where your work was criticized by a co-worker or team member. What happened? How did you handle it?

Give an example of a situation when you asked a team member for help.

Values and Ethics

Tell me about a time when you faced an ethical or moral dilemma. (Examples could include: being asked to do something you didn't agree with, or against hospital/unit policy; a friend who asked you to help them cheat on a school test or hospital competency exam; a co-worker who asked you to remain silent about their medication administration error).

Nurses have access to confidential materials and information. Describe a situation when you maintained the confidentiality of patient information or materials.

Tell me about a time you had to defend an unpopular position or one that you didn't personally agree with. (Charge nurses or RNs in supervisory positions may be confronted with this dilemma. If you're applying for a job with supervisory responsibilities, you may be asked a question like this one).

Clinical Based Behavioral Questions

Give an example of the first time you performed a procedure/treatment that you had never done before. What did you do? How did you prepare?

Tell me about a time when you had to rapidly change your priorities.

Describe a positive clinical experience you've had.

Describe a negative clinical experience you've had.

Tell me about an emergency patient situation you participated in and how you handled it.

Screening Interviews

"Know your message and no matter what is asked,
be sure you get your intended message across."

Ada Sue Hinshaw, PhD, RN, FAAN

Before we dive any deeper into preparation for formal interviews, I would be remiss if I didn't mention screening interviews. Screening interviews are an important component of the job application process, yet many job candidates don't even realize when they're participating in a screening interview. Success in the screening interview will almost certainly propel you into the formal interview process. On the other hand, if you don't make a positive impression during the screening interview, you probably won't be invited to participate in a formal interview.

The Purpose of Screening Interviews

Once you've submitted your application, resume and cover letter, your paperwork will be examined to see if you meet the minimum qualifications for the position. This task is often performed by the nurse recruiter or Human Resources department staff. Minimum qualifications could include: RN licensure, a specified minimum number of years of experience, specific certifications, etc.

After the candidates not meeting the minimum criteria are eliminated, the remaining applications will be screened further to identify the most promising prospects. Before moving to a formal interview, the top applicants will often go through a screening interview process.

Usually conducted by telephone, the screening interview is utilized to verify qualifications, gauge the applicant's interest in the position and ascertain whether the candidate should be invited to a formal interview.

Depending upon the organization, screening interviews may be conducted by the nurse recruiter, Human Resources department staff, the hiring manager or their designee.

The screening interview will usually go something like this:

Someone representing the employer will telephone you to "discuss" your job application. They may provide more information about the position and what's expected, along with information about the organization. Then they may ask you a few questions, informally: Tell me about yourself. Why are you interested in this position? What are you doing now? This is another situation where being ready to recite a brief summary of your qualifications will come in very handy.

This exchange often seems very casual and friendly—but make no mistake about it—anytime you interact with a potential employer, you are being evaluated. In this case, it's to determine whether you should be invited to interview formally for the position. If you impress the person conducting the screening interview, they may even schedule you for an interview at that time.

While you're job hunting, always be prepared to participate in a spontaneous telephone screening interview. You never know when a recruiter or potential hiring manager might call you to discuss their open positions and determine if they should bring you in for a face-to-face interview.

The screening interview is your ticket to the formal interview process. Be prepared to present yourself positively.

Telephone Interviewing Tips

• Always be prepared—think about what you would say if a potential employer called to discuss your qualifications. Be ready to provide a short description of your background and qualifications. See Chapter 6, *Preparing for Your Job Interview* for more details.

• Have a copy of your resume handy—this will help you provide information about your qualifications. You may also want to compile a short list of major accomplishments just in case you need to refer to them.

• A copy of the job description and the organization's mission and vision may also be helpful. If you're applying for multiple jobs, review documents from various employers and write a few notes about each. Keep your documents organized for easy reference. This will help you more effectively discuss a specific job and organization if you receive an impromptu telephone call.

• Speak slowly, clearly and concisely—answer questions you're asked, but don't ramble. Be purposeful with what you say.

• Smile when you're talking on the telephone—your positive attitude will come through in your tone of voice.

• Have a pen and paper with you—you may need to take notes or write down a telephone number or contact information.

• Don't talk to the potential employer while you're driving, or in a restaurant or other public place. The noise and distractions often are a turn-off for the interviewer. For example, a colleague of mine set up a screening interview with a potential employee. When she called the candidate at the scheduled time, the applicant was driving to their job—they had scheduled the screening interview during their morning commute to work. After having trouble hearing the conversation, and being disconnected during the call, the interviewer crossed this candidate off her list and moved on to the next one. If you receive a call while driving, pull into a parking lot so that you can talk without distraction. If you're in a public place, move outside or to an area where you can hear better and talk freely.

• If this time is inconvenient—ask if you can set a time to talk. Make sure you re-schedule for later that day, or within the next few days. But only do this if it's really necessary.

• Reiterate your interest in the position and ask when formal interviews will be scheduled.

• Thank the caller for contacting you and taking the time to discuss the job.

The Bottom Line

Every time you interact with a potential employer—you are being evaluated. Always be prepared to present yourself positively.

Interviewers and Their Styles

"Be appropriate! Be bold! Be courageous!"

Vernice Ferguson, MA, RN, FAAN, FRCN

The interviewer sets the tone for the interview. If they're tense, your tension will increase. If they're relaxed, it will be much easier for you to relax. A good interviewer will make you feel calm and will skillfully bring out your best during the interview.

Unfortunately, not every interviewer is experienced or has received training in the art of conducting interviews. This chapter will help you develop strategies to effectively get your message across despite the skill of your interviewer.

Different Types of Interviewers

In the pages that follow, I will describe seven basic types of interviewers and how best to communicate with them. Remember, these are generalizations—although this may be someone's predominant style, no one fits totally into one particular mold or category.

The Skilled, Experienced Interviewer—they are calm, relaxed and in control of the interview. They make you feel at ease, so that you'll reveal your true self to them. The interview will feel more like a dialogue, rather than a question and answer session. They will keep the discussion on track, and not allow the job candidate to stray too far from the outcomes the interviewer wants to achieve. If you're a strong candidate and can communicate well, you will often thrive with this type of interviewer.

The Friend—friendly, amiable, with a good sense of humor, this interviewer sets a casual, laid-back atmosphere for the interview. Often, the goal is to make you feel so relaxed and at ease that you'll let your guard down and reveal information you may not normally expose. But beware—no matter how friendly the interviewer or casual the atmosphere, this is still an interview. To get the job, you must excel. Don't be lulled into a false sense of security causing you to reveal information you intended to keep to yourself. On the flip side, don't engage in so much friendly banter that you fail to get your message across.

The Talker—these interviewers spend so much time talking about themselves and their accomplishments that you have little time to talk about yourself and your qualifications. This can be very frustrating as you feel your interview time ticking by. You must be a polite listener, but look for opportunities or common ground so that you can jump into the conversation and interject positive points about yourself and your abilities. Ask questions selectively—you don't want to encourage more talking on the interviewer's part and less on yours.

The Inquisitor—fires questions at you, one after the other. No real dialogue, just question and answer. At times you feel like you're being cross-examined by a prosecuting attorney, rather than discussing your qualifications with a potential employer. If this is the way the interviewer likes to take in information, don't try to interject small talk—just stick to the facts. However, if the questions are coming at you too rapidly for your comfort, slightly pause before you answer to slow the pace a little. This will also give you time to think about your answers. You don't want to answer questions so quickly that you make unnecessary mistakes.

The Unemotional Interviewer—this person is very concrete and data driven, and doesn't feel comfortable sharing emotions and feelings. You usually won't be able to interpret their body language because they reveal so little. If the interviewer seems to be focused on data, make sure you provide some facts and figures when answering questions and telling stories. For instance, if they ask you for an example of a patient who was positively impacted by your actions, choose a scenario where you can include some tangible data, such as vital signs, nursing diagnosis and length of stay.

The Unprepared Interviewer—this type of interviewer doesn't have questions planned and probably hasn't reviewed your resume and application prior to the interview. You know this, because they spend the first part of the interview studying your paperwork. This is a very poor interview style, because it's difficult to compare candidates effectively and fairly if they're not all asked the same basic questions. Be that as it may, if you find yourself in this type of situation, try as tactfully as you can to take control of the interview. When a question is asked of you, answer it to the best of your ability, and then try to segway to another positive point about yourself related to the original question. The unprepared interviewer will often concede control of the interview to the job candidate. So if you're in this situation, don't wait passively for conditions to improve. As much as possible, take control and focus on communicating your strengths.

The Multi-Tasker—this person is easily distracted by other tasks and commitments. If you're meeting in their office, they'll often glance at their e-mail, text messages or papers on their desk. Their attention span is short. This can be exasperating, because when you're speaking, it may seem like they're not paying attention to you. Don't take it personally—this doesn't necessarily mean they're not interested in hiring you. Keep your answers as succinct as possible. Bring them back to the conversation by sporadically asking them questions.

Although a poor interviewer can make your interview experience difficult, by using good communication skills, you can turn a potentially negative situation into a positive one. Try to interact with the interviewer in the style you think is congruent with theirs. This will help get your message across more effectively.

Additionally, if the interviewer is the department manager, you're getting a glimpse at the communication style and work habits of your potential new boss. Not only are they interviewing you—but you are also interviewing them, to ensure that the job is a good fit for you. Always ask yourself if this person's style is congruent with your own.

The Bottom Line

Know what you want to accomplish in the interview. What are the key points you really want to get across? Look for every opportunity to score these points. If you're in control of yourself—acting, rather than reacting—then the interviewer's style or tactics won't negatively affect you. Even if the road is rocky, you'll find your way!

The Day of the Interview Has Arrived!

"I don't think it's possible for anyone to be over-prepared in communication skills; this contributes greatly to professional success."

Margaret McClure, EdD, RN, FAAN

You've researched the organization. You've reviewed clinical information about the types of patients on the unit. You've been practicing your responses to interview questions. Finally, the day of the interview has arrived. All your hard work and preparation is about to pay off! You'll still be nervous, but you'll go to the interview feeling more confident and better prepared to answer questions, discuss your qualifications and most importantly—market yourself to your potential employer.

This chapter will describe strategies to boost your success during the interview.

What to Wear

Unless you wear a tuxedo or ball gown, the general rule is that you can never be overdressed for a job interview. Always project a neat and professional appearance. No jeans, scrubs or casual clothes—even if you currently work in the department that's interviewing you. I've seen instances where current employees are much too casual when interviewing for positions on their units. Because they work there, they think it's a done deal that they'll get the job. Several have been very disappointed that they didn't take their interview more seriously.

The only exception to wearing scrubs or patient care garb would be if you currently work in the department and your interview is scheduled during your shift. However for several reasons, I strongly recommend that, whenever possible, you schedule this interview on a day off. First of all, by working on the day of your interview, your concentration will be split between the pressures of the job and your upcoming meeting. During the interview, you may be thinking about a difficult patient you want to return to, or some other pressing duties needing your attention. Your performance during the interview will be much better if you're free of these distractions.

Being a current employee of the department and/or organization definitely has its advantages and disadvantages during the hiring process. On the plus side, your manager and fellow team members already know your work habits, personality and ability to mesh with the team. If they have a positive impression of you, it will certainly give you an edge over other job candidates.

On the flip side, however, as an employee of the department, your co-workers see you in a certain role. Sometimes it's difficult for them to envision you in another role. For example, you may be a nursing assistant on the Respiratory Unit who recently graduated from nursing school. Now you're applying for an RN job. It may be difficult for your manager and co-workers to picture you in the RN role because they think of you as "our nursing assistant." Or, you're a staff RN who is now applying for a supervisory position. Your peers may have difficulty thinking of you in that role because you're "one of us."

Attending the job interview during your shift, wearing your department badge and work clothes, perpetuates this image and bias. Attending the interview dressed in professional clothing on a day off from work will help project the image that you have additional dimensions, talents and potential.

I'm not saying that you downplay your current role on the unit. On the contrary—every chance you get during the interview—remind them how your experience and knowledge of the organization puts you ahead of your competitors. However, you also want them to see that you have other facets—including skills and abilities they may not have considered. Interviewing on a day off and wearing professional clothing will help project this image.

What to Wear?

All clothes—neat, clean, wrinkle-free.

Men
- Suit, collared shirt and tie, preferably a dark suit. If you don't have a suit—then wear dress slacks, collared shirt, tie and jacket/blazer.

- Shoes to match your slacks. Make sure they're polished and scuff-free.

Women
- Suit—skirt or slacks with matching jacket and blouse. If you don't have a suit, then wear a skirt or dress slacks with a complementary blouse and blazer; or a dress with jacket, blazer or nice cardigan.

- Shoes should be conservative—closed-toed pumps or flats and hosiery. Most health care organizations don't allow their employees to wear open-toed shoes, so don't wear them to the interview.

Don't Wear (some apply to both men and women)
- Excessively high heels, sneakers/tennis shoes, flip flops, beach shoes or any other shoes that don't appear professional.

- Jeans, shorts, t-shirts, scrubs

Also Avoid:
- Tattoos—if you have large or multiple tattoos—cover them. Many facilities will require you to keep them hidden when on the job.

- Excessive jewelry—especially large and/or multiple earrings, and facial or other body jewelry. As above, in many health care settings, you won't be permitted to wear these.

- Excessively long nails, artificial nails and heavy cologne/perfume— again, most health care employers don't allow these.

  Show that you understand the rules by not wearing them during the interview.

What to Bring With You

Extra copies of your resume—you never know how many people will participate in the interview. They should already have copies of your resume, but bring four copies just to be prepared.

Performance Evaluation—this is optional. If you have an evaluation from work or school, especially if you were rated highly, bring at least two copies with you. If there's an opportunity, you may be able to smoothly integrate it into your interview. That's why you want at least one copy for the interviewer and one for you to refer to. If you don't have an opportunity to introduce it during the interview, leave a copy with the interviewer(s) at the conclusion of the meeting.

If you're not ranked highly in most categories covered in the evaluation, don't bring it to the interview. I once interviewed a job candidate who performed favorably during the interview. When she provided a copy of her performance appraisal from her current job, I was surprised to see that she ranked average or below average in nearly every category. I didn't ask her to provide this information— she volunteered it. She was one of the top contenders before I saw her performance evaluation. After reviewing it, I decided not to offer her the job.

Letters of recommendation—also optional. If you have one or two letters of recommendation from employers and/or teachers, you can also bring a few copies with you. This is more important for a new graduate and usually not necessary for an experienced nurse (unless of course you were asked for letters of recommendation).

Pen and paper to take notes—you may want to jot down some notes during the interview. Limit yourself to key points you want to remember. Don't take excessive notes.

Packaging your documents—if you're going to provide the interviewer with multiple documents, such as a past evaluation and letters of recommendation, place these documents along with your resume into a presentation folder or portfolio. This will be a nice, neat package you can present to the interviewer. But, only include a few key documents—don't try to cram in a bunch of materials.

Look for opportunities during the interview to introduce these documents. For example, as a new grad you may say: "I feel I really excelled in my externship/final practicum. In fact, I'd like to share with you a letter of recommendation from my preceptor."

Obtaining Letters of Recommendation

When selecting people to write letters of recommendation for you, choose those who can best comment on your skills, abilities, work habits, motivation, values and personal attributes. Letters should come from professional and educational sources, rather than personal ones. This can include current and former employers, faculty and professional/ community organizations.

Ask people who know you best for these references. When I was a nursing student, I once asked an instructor I admired for a letter of recommendation. After I read the letter, I realized that she didn't know me well enough to recommend me. The letter was vague and didn't include my key attributes. I then asked another faculty member who was more aware of my skills. I threw out the first letter and used the second one.

Give the individual plenty of time to complete your letter of recommendation. This is especially true for faculty who are often inundated with requests as the end of the school term approaches. Assist the person by providing them with a brief list of your major accomplishments.

Some hiring managers will request letters of recommendation in sealed envelopes with the reference's signature over the seal. If this is the case, ask the recommender for a copy of the letter they submitted, so that you know what they're saying about you. Most people are willing to provide this.

Arriving for Your Interview

Be on time! Remember, employers are looking for dependable and reliable people. Being late for your interview sends a HUGE negative message, and you start your interview with one strike against you. Additionally, there are probably other interviews scheduled after yours. If you're late, many interviewers won't give you extra time, but will cut the interview short when the next candidate arrives.

So, allow yourself plenty of time to get to the interview early. In large hospitals or health care organizations, parking may be time-consuming, you'll need to locate the room where the interview will take place, there may be excessive traffic or road construction on your way to the interview, etc.

If something unforeseen happens and you're running late, call the interviewer and let them know. Ask if they'd prefer you to re-schedule. Reiterate that this was an unforeseen occurrence, and you are still very interested in the job.

If the interviewer isn't available (possibly conducting another interview), leave a message with whomever answers the telephone. Be sure to get their name. Also leave a message on the manager's voicemail so there's a timed record of your call. If you weren't able to speak to the manager about rescheduling, get to the interview as quickly as possible. If you arrive more than ten minutes late, explain the situation to the interviewer and ask if they would prefer that you reschedule.

It's all about accommodating your potential employer—not about them accommodating you!

Before You Meet the Interviewer

• Visit the restroom and freshen up

• Wash your hands so that they're fresh and dry when you shake the interviewer's hand

• Carry some tissue with you in case you need to wipe your nose

• Take a drink of water, so your throat isn't dry

• Pop a breath mint in your mouth

• Take a deep breath and try to relax

Greeting the Interviewer

First impressions are extremely important. Greet your interviewer positively. If you're sitting—stand up. Smile, make eye contact, say hello with enthusiasm, call them by name and shake their hand. Unless they have an injury or noticeable physical problem with their hand, grasp it firmly. "Wimpy" handshakes are a negative for most interviewers and hiring managers.

A firm handshake, eye contact and positive greeting tells the interviewer you're confident, enthusiastic and comfortable communicating with strangers. The greeting sets the tone for the interview.

How to Greet an Interview Panel

This really depends upon the physical set up of the room. If there's enough space to approach each panel member, shake their hands as you're being introduced. If the space is small and it would be awkward to shake each panel member's hand, don't do it. In that case, as each panel member is being introduced, make eye contact and greet them.

Moving Through the Interview

Take a deep breath and try to relax—the interview is about to begin. The interview usually starts with an overview of how the meeting will be conducted. Sometimes an explanation of the job is also offered. Listen carefully; this may give you insight into the type of employee they're looking for. Interviews are typically 30 – 45 minutes, sometimes longer if the job is supervisory or has a wide range of responsibilities. If an interview goes over the stated time, this could be a positive indicator that they like you and want to learn more about you. It could also mean the interviewer is inexperienced and unskilled at wrapping up the meeting—but let's think positively!

Interview Dos

- Dress professionally

- Turn off your cell phone (that's off—not vibrate!)

- Greet the interviewer positively and with enthusiasm

- Smile often

- Shake hands firmly and warmly

- Make eye contact when answering questions

- Let your enthusiasm show through

- Be honest

- Think before answering

- Tell stories and give examples to illustrate your key points

- Thank the interviewer(s) for taking the time to meet with you

Interview Don'ts

- Arrive late

- Bring your Starbuck's latte

- Chew gum

- Have a casual attitude

- Let a cell phone ring or answer a call

- Slouch during the interview

- Speak negatively about a current or past employer

When Answering Questions

Listen carefully to what the interviewer is asking, and answer the question. I've conducted several interviews where the candidate provides information they think is important, but doesn't answer my question. Remember, the interviewer knows what they're looking for. The questions they ask are designed to help them determine if you're the right person for the job. Help them by answering the questions they ask. *Exception:* If they ask you an illegal question. *More about illegal questions later in this chapter.*

If you're not quite sure what they're asking for, clarify the question. Ask the interviewer to repeat or re-phrase the question. Or, pose a clarifying question to ensure you understand what they're asking you.

If you don't have an immediate answer to their question, ask for a moment to think about it. Especially with behavioral questions where the interviewer is looking for an example from your past, you may need to think for a moment for the most appropriate situation to illustrate your point. A little silence is acceptable—but let the interviewer know that you're thinking about their question.

This is where your interview practice will pay off—you'll be able to think of an answer more effectively. You'll also be more calm and confident as you formulate your answer.

Watch body language—yours and the interviewer's. In Chapter 6, *Preparing for the Interview*, we talked about the importance of body language, and why your body language must align with the verbal message you're delivering. Hopefully, you practiced your answers in front of a mirror or with a friend. Remember what you practiced.

It's also important to watch the body language of the people who are interviewing you. Look for clues to confirm, refine or modify your tactics. Here are some examples:

- If people are nodding their heads at your answer—it's a good bet they approve or agree with what you're saying.

- If someone is frowning or appears that they don't understand your answer, rephrase your response. It's also acceptable to ask: "Did that answer your question?" Or: "Would you like me to clarify further?" Don't ask this for every question, only when you think clarification may be needed.

- If it appears the interviewer(s) aren't paying close attention to you, then your answers may be too long. Remember, you're striving to deliver thorough answers, but your answers must also be concise and to the point.

Be Honest. Throughout this book, I've stressed the importance of honesty. Be honest about your skills, experience and abilities. Especially in a tough job market, it's tempting to tell some "white lies" about your qualifications in order to make yourself more attractive to potential employers.

Don't succumb to this urge. In these situations, honesty really is the best policy. Employers are looking for honest, reliable employees—people they can trust and build a lasting employment relationship with. If they perceive you're being dishonest or exaggerating your qualifications, you won't get the job. Furthermore, they may alert their Human Resources department about you. This will make it difficult for you to ever get a job in their organization.

Before making a final job offer, employers verify licensure and often certifications. So, if you say you have a current certification, you'd better be prepared to show proof. In my health care management roles, I've seen job offers rescinded and new employees terminated because they presented false certifications to match the information they provided on their resumes and/or in job interviews.

Okay so you don't have much job experience and your skills are new. But you're excited about being a nurse. You want to care for patients and be a part of the organization. Show this to your potential employer. Emphasize the skills, experience and accomplishments you've achieved so far. Let your enthusiasm, drive, values and integrity make up for your lack of experience. Always emphasize that you want to expand your knowledge and improve your skills.

The information you discuss in the interview must match your resume. Continuing our discussion above, make sure the points you emphasize during the interview aren't in conflict with the information on your resume, cover letter or any other materials you provided to your potential employer. If the facts don't jive, it's a red flag that your information may be false.

Remember, the key to effective marketing—whether you're selling a product, service or yourself as a potential employee, is to keep the message simple and consistent. Your resume tells a story. Your cover letter calls attention to the highlights of the resume. And finally, during the job interview you tell the stories to bring home the messages you began with your resume and cover letter.

Frequently Asked Question
Answering Questions During a Panel Interview

When someone on the interview panel asks me a question, should I make eye contact only with that person or the entire panel?

Answer: Begin and end your answer by making eye contact with the person who asked the question. In between, while answering the question, scan the entire panel. Not only are you acknowledging them, but you're also looking for cues in their body language.

Inappropriate Interview Questions

Provisions of the *Equal Employment Opportunities Act* and other employment laws prohibit potential employers from asking personal questions related to race, religion, marital status, sexual orientation, children, physical disabilities, political ideologies and other personal topics.

Illegal questions about the topics listed above are supposed to be off limits. Unfortunately, they sometimes creep into job interviews. Most of the time, it's because the interviewer is inexperienced and doesn't know they cannot ask these types of questions. At other times, the interviewer may have such concerns about an issue, that they knowingly take the risk of asking illegal questions during the interview.

Through properly phrased questions, a skilled interviewer can usually garner the information they need without asking an inappropriate question. See the box on page 100 for samples of legal and illegal questions.

Handling Illegal Questions

How should you handle an inappropriate question? Should you answer it, knowing it shouldn't have been asked? Do you point out to the interviewer that the question is illegal?

It really depends on the situation and your comfort level. The final decision is yours. If you want to answer the question, then go ahead.

Illegal Question	Legal Question
Do your religious beliefs preclude you from working weekends?	Our department is open seven days per week. Every staff member is expected to work two weekends per month. Is there anything that would prevent you from working weekend shifts?
I noticed you limping when you walked into the room. Is that a permanent condition? Are you going to be able to stand and walk for long periods of time?	According to our job description, our nurses must be able to stand for long periods of time and do a lot of walking. Is there anything that would prevent you from doing this?
Is your husband in the military or in a job where you might be relocated soon?	Due to the long orientation and training period for new RNs on our unit, we will ask those we hire to commit to staying on the unit for a minimum of two years. Is there any reason why you couldn't or wouldn't make that commitment? *
Have you ever been arrested?	Have you ever been convicted of a crime?

* As a side note, your potential employer can ask you for a commitment to stay on the unit for a minimum of two years, but this is not legally binding. The hope is that if you commit, you will keep your promise. Although the employer can't force you to stay for two years, if they are providing a sign-on bonus, paying off your student loans, or awarding other financial incentives above your salary, they can specify that you receive incremental payments of these incentives throughout the two-year period. Therefore, if you choose to leave prior to the two years, you would not receive the full incentives.

If you don't feel comfortable answering the question, don't do it. But, be aware that calling attention to an illegal question probably won't endear you to the interviewer, especially if they are a member of an interview panel. They may feel that you've just embarrassed them in front of the group. Therefore, you must handle the situation delicately.

If you don't want to answer, then try to ascertain the underlying employment-related reason why they asked you this question. For example, let's say you're asked if you are a parent with young children. This is obviously an inappropriate question. Quickly think about why the interviewer may have asked you this question. The most logical reason is that they're trying to gauge your reliability. Generally speaking, single parents with small children have more unforeseen emergencies which may impact their absentee rate and punctuality.

Once you've identified what you think is the issue, you can provide an answer without revealing personal information. In this instance, you can say: "I think you're asking me this question to find out if I will show up for work as scheduled and on time. I'm very reliable and dependable. I have an excellent attendance record at my current job. If you like, I will provide my manager's contact information so that you can be reassured about my reliability."

During the interview, job candidates sometimes inadvertently bring up personal information themselves. When you introduce information about your personal life during the interview, you open the door for the interviewer to pursue that topic. This can result in an uncomfortable situation if you don't want to answer further questions about a topic you brought up in the first place.

It's best to keep the conversation focused on information related to the job and your qualifications.

For More Information About Inappropriate Questions

If you'd like more information about illegal and inappropriate interview questions and what to do about them, only an expert in employment law can give you legal advice about a specific issue or occurrence. For additional general information, visit the *Equal Employment Opportunity Commission* website at www.eeoc.gov.

Wrapping Up the Interview

In preparation for the interview, you researched the organization and/or department. During the interview, you learned more about the job. As the interview is wrapping up, ask some questions of your own. Not only will this provide you with more information, but it shows your continued interest in the position. If you can't think of job or department specific questions to ask, here are general topic areas from which you can build questions:

- Unit/department culture

- Work schedule/expectations

- Opportunities for education and professional development

- Orientation, training and preceptor policy

As the interview is reaching its conclusion, ask the interviewer when they expect to make their decision. Request permission to contact them if you haven't heard any news within the specified timeframe. Reiterate that you are very interested in the position and ask if there's any additional information you can provide to help them make their decision.

Finally, thank the interviewer or panel for taking the time to meet with you. If possible, get the business card(s) of the interviewer(s). Hopefully someone will escort you to the door. This will be a good opportunity for you to shake hands once more.

Take a deep breath and let out a sigh of relief. You've survived the interview!

The Bottom Line

Advanced preparation, awareness of body language and making a positive first impression are keys to success in the job interview. Always project a professional image—from the clothes you wear to the way you answer interview questions.

Notes:

Following-Up After the Interview

"Overcoming the fear of taking a risk and failing is one of life's most valuable lessons."

Faye Abdullah, EdD, ScD, RN, FAAN

After the interview comes one of the most difficult periods in your job search—waiting to hear if you got the job!

Even though this period is predominately a waiting game, there are still some strategies you can utilize to get the attention of your potential employer. Additionally, this is a time to analyze your performance in order to improve your job interviewing skills.

Thank-You Messages

Within 24 hours of your interview, send a thank-you to the interviewer and/or members of the interview panel (that's why you got their cards before leaving the interview).

Keep your thank-you message short, but include the following components:

- Thanks to the interviewer(s) for taking time out of their busy schedule to meet with you.

- A statement reaffirming that you're very interested in the position.

- Key points emphasizing why you're the right person for the job.

For example:

"I was very impressed with your unit's interventional cardiology program. Cardiac care is my passion, that's why I chose cardiac telemetry for my externship. I believe I can positively contribute to the work of your department."

OR

"As you know, I have eight years experience caring for post-op patients on the surgical unit. I'm very motivated to take my skills to the next level. That's why I applied for your position in the Surgical ICU. I'm eager to learn and want to become a member of your team."

• Ask if there's any more information you can provide to help them make their decision. This may spark a call or e-mail from the manager to clarify a fact or learn more about you.

Formats for Thank-You Messages

Should your thank-you message be an e-mail, formal letter or handwritten note? Here are some positives and negatives for each of these methods:

E-Mail—will arrive in a very timely manner. This is especially important if you know the manager is planning to make a decision rapidly. E-mail gives you the flexibility to add any key points you wished you'd mentioned during the interview. In the case of an interview panel, you can compose a basic message and customize it for each individual. *Potential downside:* managers are inundated by e-mails. Your e-mail message could get lost in the hiring manager's *Inbox.* Also, because this is the easiest way to respond, it shows less effort on your part than the following two thank-you methods.

Formal Letter—this is a formal thank-you message set up as a business letter. Ideally, the stationary and envelope you use should match your resume paper. As in the e-mail message, you can easily add a few key points about your qualifications. In the case of an interview panel, compose a basic message and customize it for each recipient. The formal letter shows more effort than sending an e-mail. *Potential downside:* if the employer is going to make a decision quickly, this letter might not reach them in time.

Handwritten Note—handwritten on a card or stationary. This is the most time-consuming strategy, therefore, it shows the most effort.

Possible downsides: as with formal letters, your note may not reach the manager before a hiring decision is made. Also, because this note is handwritten, it should be short. As a result, you won't have as much space to highlight key points about your qualifications. And to utilize this method, you must also have neat, legible handwriting.

Which method should you use?

Once again, it boils down to your audience and the circumstances. Generally speaking, managers who are over 40 years of age prefer formal letters or handwritten notes. Younger managers tend to be more comfortable with electronic communication. As a result, e-mail would probably be their communication preference. During the interview, notice if the interviewer has an *iPhone, Blackberry*, etc. This will give you a hint about whether or not they check their e-mail often. If yes, an e-mail message would probably be most effective.

You must also consider the circumstances. If you really want to stress some key information about your qualifications, an e-mail or formal letter is preferable. Furthermore, if you know the employer is making a decision within a few days after the interview—e-mail is the best option to make sure the message arrives on time. If you would prefer to send a formal letter or handwritten note, you can hand deliver it to the unit to make sure the message arrives on time.

No matter what format you choose, I can't emphasize enough, the importance of sending a thank-you message. First of all, it's proper etiquette—someone took the time to interview you and consider you for a job. Of course you should thank them. In addition, it gives you one more chance to connect with the people making the hiring decision. If you want the job, you can't afford to pass up this opportunity.

I once interviewed for a position, and got the job. On my first day of work, my new manager told me that I was the only job candidate who sent her a thank-you message. Although this wasn't the main reason she hired me, she said that my note made me stand out from the others she interviewed.

Today, a growing number of people are recognizing the importance of thank-you messages. If you don't send one, then you may stand out—in a negative way.

Second Interviews

Sometimes, organizations will schedule multiple interviews before making their decision. There are several situations where multiple interviews may be conducted. Here are some examples:

• A manager may prefer to conduct the initial interviews to narrow the field to the top three or four candidates. The next step is a panel interview with departmental staff to give them a voice in hiring their co-workers.

• Conversely, the interview panel may consist of the supervisor and staff members. The panel narrows the field to a few candidates. The manager interviews the top candidates and makes the final decision.

• In another situation, there are two job candidates who would both be excellent additions to the team. Unfortunately, there is only one open position. A second interview might be scheduled to take another look at these candidates before making the final decision.

Multiple interviews are also more likely for key jobs such as management positions, clinical educators or other specialist roles.

If you're called in for a second interview—celebrate that you've gotten this far in the process! Then once again, prepare, prepare, prepare for the second interview. Review your original research notes from your prep session for the first interview.

Critically review your performance during the first interview. Were there any questions you could have answered better? Think about some of the key questions you were asked. Are there other scenarios or examples to better illustrate your strengths in these areas? Finally, can you anticipate what they may ask you in the next interview?

Ask who will be conducting the second interview. If new people are handling the interview, you may get some of the original questions you were asked during the first interview. However, if the same people are interviewing you, then it's a good bet you'll be asked new questions. As you prepare, try to anticipate these questions and practice your answers as you did for the first interview.

Other Strategies While You're Waiting

If you've built a relationship with the nurse recruiter, contact them and let them know how the interview went. Reiterate your interest in the open position and the organization. This is a courtesy as well as an indicator of your professionalism. The recruiter may contact the hiring manager to put in a good word for you. If it turns out you aren't offered the job, you'll want the recruiter to be on the lookout for other jobs within the organization. Your demonstrated professionalism and positive relationship with the recruiter are great assets.

Continue Your Job Search

While you're waiting to hear if you got the job, continue your job search. Many job applicants put their job hunt on hold while they wait and hope. This wastes valuable time and will prolong your job search.

This job may be extremely important to you, but you don't know where it falls on the hiring manager's list of priorities. If their need is acute and immediate—they'll want to fill the position as soon as possible. On the other hand, if their department is adequately staffed, day-to-day demands may push the job opening to the bottom of their priority list. You don't want to waste time while you wait for a decision.

You may think this is your ideal job. One you would snatch immediately if it is offered to you. But there are other jobs out there, too. Continue to network, search job sites, submit applications and participate in other job interviews. If it turns out you don't get the job you interviewed for, then you've already made great strides toward the next opportunity. Remember, your job search is fluid. Don't be passive—take control and continue to move forward. Eventually, your efforts will pay off.

Stay in Contact with the Nurse Recruiter

Just because the interview is over—don't stop your efforts to market yourself within the organization. Contact the recruiter and let them know how the interview went. Make sure they know you are very interested in this position, as well as other jobs within the organization if you're not offered this one.

What if I'm offered another job while I'm waiting to hear about this one?

Then, you're very lucky. This tells you that you have qualifications employers are looking for. But, what about your decision?

Let's set the stage. You interviewed for Job A, and you think it's a job you'd really like. You also interviewed for Job B. This would be a good job, too, but you'd prefer Job A. The problem is that Job B Employer has just called and offered you Job B.

You don't have to provide an answer immediately. Thank Job B Employer for the job offer—be sure to say this enthusiastically. Tell Job B Employer you need some time to think about it. Promise to give your answer in a few days. If this isn't acceptable to Job B Employer, then negotiate an acceptable date and time.

In the meantime, call Job A Employer and inform them that you've received a job offer from another organization. Although the job offer is a good one, you'd prefer Job A. If you're one of the top candidates, this may be enough to prompt a decision from Job A Employer. They may offer you the position on the spot. If they don't offer you Job A, very politely and respectfully ask for a decision by a certain date and time (before you must give your answer to Job B Employer).

If Job A Employer remains noncommittal about getting back to you within your timeframe, you might not be a top contender for the position. Or, Job A Employer may be having a difficult time reaching a decision. Ask Job A Employer if they consider you one of the top candidates for the position. This conversation may help you decide whether you really want Job A and if this manager is someone you want to work for.

If you don't hear back from Job A Employer by your deadline—you have a difficult decision to make: do you take the sure thing, or hold out for the job you'd prefer?

There is no right or wrong answer to this question. It's your decision. But, I do want to remind you of the old saying: "A bird in the hand is worth two in the bush!" Take a hard, honest look at what your prospects would be if you let Job B go by, and subsequently didn't receive an offer for Job A.

Part of this decision may depend upon whether you already have a job. If you could see yourself remaining in your current position while you continue your job search, then you may want to hold out for Job A. On the other hand, if you're a new grad or an unemployed experienced RN, the bird in the hand—Job B will probably look more attractive. In the end, it's your choice to make. See the Job Assessment Tool on page 115. This tool will help you organize the information needed to make an informed decision.

The Bottom Line

After the interview—be proactive. Stay in contact with the organization, but at the same time, continue your job search. Work your contacts, apply for other positions and participate in other interviews.

You Got the Job!

"All our dreams can come true - if we have the
courage to pursue them!"

Walt Disney

Your cell phone is ringing. It's the manager who interviewed you last week, and they're offering you the job...CONGRATULATIONS! But before you say, yes, there are some points to consider. This chapter will help you determine what questions to ask to ensure success in your new job.

I'd Like to Offer You This Position...

These are great words to hear when you're looking for a job. If you're currently unemployed, a new nurse graduate or you're looking for a ticket out of your current employment situation; your immediate inclination will be to shout: "Yes, I'll take it!"

Before you do, here are some questions to ask and points to clarify prior to accepting the position:

Orientation and training—this is especially important for a new graduate RN. Is there a new grad training program? A residency program? How long is the orientation period? Does the organization have an education department? Can I attend classes to build my skills and knowledge? What if I need more? As a new grad, you'll want adequate orientation, training and access to educational opportunities to help you learn your new role and responsibilities and grow in the position. Hopefully, you discussed this during the job interview. Make sure you're accepting a job in a department and organization committed to helping you succeed.

This is also important if you're an experienced RN who is offered a position in a new area of practice. You want adequate orientation and training to ensure your success. Additionally, you'll want access to educational opportunities to continue to grow in your career.

Shift, hours, etc.—are they offering you the position you discussed in the interview? Sometimes people interview for a full time position, and are then offered a part time one. Or, you may have interviewed for the day shift and now you're being offered a spot on the night shift. Make sure you know all the facts about the position before saying yes.

Salary—where do you fall on the salary range? A new graduate will probably start at the lowest point on the salary range. That's standard. But what if you're an entry-level, master's prepared RN, or have some special skills and experience? You may be able to negotiate a higher salary. I only recommend this if you have special education or experience which sets you apart from other candidates. Although Human Resources staff usually determines the rate of pay, the hiring manager occasionally has some leeway to negotiate a higher salary—if the increase can be justified.

If you're an experienced RN, make sure the point you're placed on the salary range is appropriate for your qualifications. If you don't think so, you may be able to negotiate. Note: If you're offered a position in a unionized facility, the salary structure is very concrete. You probably won't be able to negotiate a higher salary. However, it never hurts to clarify how your salary level was calculated.

Benefits—your new manager can tell you in general about benefits. You can also get more detailed information from Human Resources.

Do nurses have a voice in patient care decisions?—it may be important for you to work in an organization where nurses participate on committees, impact quality improvement processes and have a say in decisions affecting patient care. If this is a factor that will influence your job performance and satisfaction, be sure to ask about it.

Any other arrangements you discussed during the interview— this could be attendance at an upcoming conference or educational program, guaranteed time off next month to take the cruise you've already paid for, or this Christmas off to attend a family reunion in another state. Whatever the arrangement you and the manager discussed previously, remind them of it and make sure they still agree to it.

Offer Letter

In many organizations, you'll receive a letter outlining the provisions of your job offer. This will be signed by you and a representative of the organization. It should include salary, hours, terms of employment and any special arrangements and agreements between you and the hiring manager. If there's something in the offer letter that isn't what you believe you agreed to—don't sign the letter. And don't ignore the issue. Right now, you're thrilled to be offered the job. But down the road, after you've been working for the organization awhile, you may harbor some unresolved negative feelings about this issue. This can affect your attitude and level of job satisfaction. Discuss the discrepancy with your new manager before you begin working, and request a revised copy of your offer letter. In the long run, you'll be happy you did!

I Just Want a Job!

Should I accept a position in an organization or area of practice I'm not interested in?

Only you can ultimately make that decision. However in a tight job market, if you're a new graduate, it may be better to accept a position in order to build your resume, experience and skills so you can later qualify for a more desirable job.

If you're an experienced nurse—it really depends upon your financial situation, whether you currently have a job and what your prospects are for other positions. If you recently began your search and are aware of several jobs you're qualified for, it's not as big of a risk to turn down this job. However, if you're out of work and your prospects limited, this open position will be much more attractive.

Whether you're a new RN or an experienced one, if you decide to accept a job, commit to giving it your best effort. Look for the positives— steady paycheck, chance to build or improve skills, a new team to join, educational opportunities and patients to care for.

Focusing on the positives will help build your excitement and enthusiasm for the position. If you give the job your best efforts, you may find you really like it, or you'll build a positive reference to utilize when you're ready to look for another position. Either way, stay in the role for a minimum of one year so it doesn't appear that you're a job hopper.

See the Job Assessment Tool on page 115. This tool will help you organize the information needed to make an informed decision about job offers and opportunities.

The Bottom Line

Before accepting the job, ask questions and clarify details to ensure the position, department and organization are a good fit for you. If you accept a position that isn't one of your top choices, commit to giving the job and organization your best effort.

Assessment Tool #3 - Evaluating Job Opportunities

Utilize this assessment tool to compare job offers and opportunities. Not all factors may apply to every situation, but this guide will help you organize key information in order to reach an informed decision.

Job A	Job B
Orientation and Training New grad program?	**Orientation and Training** New grad program?
Residency program?	Residency program?
What is the orientation period?	What is the orientation period?
Can the orientation period be extended if needed?	Can the orientation period be extended if needed?
Will my preceptor be one person, or several?	Will my preceptor be one person, or several?
Does the organization have an education department?	Does the organization have an education department?
Am I allowed to take classes?	Am I allowed to take classes?
Is there paid continuing education time?	Is there paid continuing education time?
Tuition reimbursement?	Tuition reimbursement?

Job A	Job B
Shift, Hours Is the job full-time or part-time? What shift am I being offered? 8, 10 or 12 hour shifts? Other?	**Shift, Hours** Is the job full-time or part-time? What shift am I being offered? 8, 10 or 12 hour shifts? Other?
Salary What is the salary? How does it compare with other organizations in the community? How often are salary increases? What factors determine the salary increase amount? What is the shift differential? (if applicable) Weekend differential?	**Salary** What is the salary? How does it compare with other organizations in the community? How often are salary increases? What factors determine the salary increase amount? What is the shift differential? (if applicable) Weekend differential?

Job A	Job B
Nursing Voice in Patient Care Decisions	**Nursing Voice in Patient Care Decisions**
Committee participation?	Committee participation?
Quality improvement projects?	Quality improvement projects?
Other?	Other?
Benefits What are the major provisions of the benefit package?	**Benefits** What are the major provisions of the benefit package?
How much do I need to contribute to cover my family? (if applicable)	How much do I need to contribute to cover my family? (if applicable)
What are the provisions of the retirement plan?	What are the provisions of the retirement plan?
Other factors Use this space to list other factors relevant to your decision...	**Other factors** Use this space to list other factors relevant to your decision...

Unfortunately, You Didn't Get the Job...

13

"There are no secrets to success. It is the result of preparation, hard work and learning from failure."

Colin Powell

Finding out you didn't get the job is a message you don't want to hear and one managers hate to deliver! Although you're disappointed, you can still make this a positive experience by learning and growing from it.

Always look for lessons to learn from your job hunting experiences. Analyze and re-analyze your resume and cover letter to seek opportunities for improvement. If you got an interview, then your resume and cover letter/message did their jobs. Replay the interview experience in your mind and look for ways you could have answered the questions better. Were there any questions you couldn't answer? How about questions you didn't anticipate? Did any of your responses elicit negative body language from the interviewer(s)? Answering these questions will help you identify areas for improvement.

You can also contact the potential employer for feedback. Who to contact will depend upon where you got stalled in the process.

You Applied for the Job, but didn't get an Interview

Contact the nurse recruiter. Tell them you're trying to improve your ability to communicate with potential employers regarding your qualifications. Although you didn't get an interview, you want to learn from the process. Politely ask why you weren't chosen for an interview. Encourage them to be honest with you. Reiterate that your goal is to more effectively communicate your qualifications to potential employers.

Maybe the recruiter will tell you it was difficult to determine your skills and abilities from your resume. If that's the case, take a critical look at your resume. As we discussed in Chapter 4, *Creating Effective Resumes*, a potential employer will initially scan resumes to ascertain a job candidate's qualifications. If your resume is confusing and/or difficult to read, you will most likely be passed by and your resume sent to the rejection pile.

Perhaps the recruiter tells you that they received 200 applications for three open positions. As a result, the hiring manager revised the selection criteria to "RNs with a minimum of two years of patient care experience." Since you're a new graduate, your resume was automatically eliminated.

Yes, this is discouraging, but at least you know the problem wasn't your resume or the way you presented yourself—it was the addition of criteria you don't meet.

Asking for Suggestions

Since you have the recruiter on the telephone, utilize this valuable time. Ask for suggestions—what can you do to be a desirable candidate for a position within their organization?

If the recruiter seems willing to help you, ask if they would review your resume and offer suggestions for improvement. But be respectful of their time—if they can't look at your resume now, perhaps they can review it later. Suggest that they call or e-mail you at their convenience, or better yet, set up an appointment for a short discussion. This continues your relationship with the recruiter and provides you with valuable feedback about your resume.

You had an Interview, but didn't get the Job

Typically, nursing managers are very busy, therefore, you may have difficulty connecting with them on the telephone. If the nurse recruiter was part of the interview team, you're more likely to get a response from the recruiter than the hiring manager.

If the recruiter wasn't involved in the interview, send an e-mail to the hiring manager. Thank them again for considering you for the position. Express your desire to improve your interview skills. Was there anything you said or did during the interview that had a negative impact? Ask for suggestions to improve your communication and interview skills.

Keep your e-mail as brief as possible. Whether you get a response will depend on the manager's time constraints and their interest in helping RNs develop professionally.

The Bottom Line

If you didn't get the job, learn from the experience in order to improve your communication and interview skills. Ask the recruiter and/or hiring manager why you didn't get the job. Use this feedback to build a stronger presence for the next job opportunity.

Staying On Track: Continuing Your Job Search

"If you are facing the right direction - all you need to do is keep on walking!"

Buddhist Saying

In a competitive job market, finding a nursing position can be a difficult and frustrating process. You may have discovered a job that seemed perfect for you, yet you never made it to the interview process because there were so many candidates. Or, you had an interview—only to learn that someone else was hired instead of you.

Throughout this book, we've talked about ways to connect with potential employers, build professional relationships, market your unique talents and abilities, create effective resumes and cover letters, prepare for job interviews and follow-up after. The information and strategies presented are meant to be guidelines you can adapt for your distinct situation. My goal is to provide you with a foundation to help you learn and grow.

These strategies for success will help you land a job—maybe not today, but soon. What's important is that you stay motivated and focused. As many recruiters and human resources professionals would say: *Make looking for a job, your job!* Devote time and energy to your job search each day.

- Look for new job postings on organizational sites and job boards.

- Contact recruiters and other resources. Find out if their organizations have current or upcoming job openings. Always ask for suggestions about where and what to try next.

- Review your resume to ensure that it's clear, concise and conveys your message effectively. As needed, adjust your resume to focus on the needs of a particular employer.

- In all interactions, present your qualifications honestly. Let your enthusiasm and passion shine through.

- Always provide a cover letter/message with all job applications, targeted to the requirements of the job and the needs of the employer.

- Refine your communication techniques and interview skills. If you need more practice in this area, consider taking a class on the subject.

Other Strategies

- Don't limit your job search only to acute care nursing positions. There are wonderful opportunities in long term care, sub-acute care, rehabilitation, outpatient clinics and the list goes on.

- Look for opportunities outside your community. Consider relocating in order to find a job that's right for you. Use the Internet to help you locate potential job prospects.

- Join a medical mission, either within the US or in another country. Not only will you build valuable skills and add to your resume, but you'll make important contacts and gain personal enrichment by providing basic nursing care to people in need. In most cases, you don't need to be an experienced RN to be part of a mission.

- Get involved in professional nursing organizations. Through networking opportunities, you'll build valuable contacts and relationships. This will help you in your current job search and throughout your career.

- Go back to school. If you have an Associate degree, work toward your Bachelor of Science in Nursing. If you're a Bachelor's prepared nurse, consider obtaining a Master's degree. There are scholarships and loan forgiveness programs available for those who agree to work for a specified amount of time in underserved areas.

Always Look for Opportunities to Expand Your Knowledge and Develop Professionally

Successful RNs recognize that life-long learning is a key component for career satisfaction and professional growth. Throughout your career, look for opportunities to expand your knowledge and education, such as attaining an advanced degree and attending conferences and continuing education programs.

Several years ago when I was manager of an education department at a small community hospital, my boss asked me to attend a two-day seminar about finding and hiring qualified employees. She wanted me to utilize this information to train and coach managers to improve their skills in selecting the best candidates for their open positions. Seeing this as an opportunity to expand my own knowledge, I agreed. I had no idea my expertise in this area would continue to grow, and years later, I would write a book on this subject. That's the wonderful benefit of education—you never know where it will take you, or what doors it will open for you!

The Bottom Line

Right now, looking for a job - is your job! Keep your job search active by utilizing the many strategies in this book. Continue to move forward and you will eventually achieve success.

The FINAL Bottom Line: Don't Give Up!

A tight nursing job market is usually a temporary symptom of an unhealthy economy. As the economy improves, more jobs will open up. RNs who delayed retirement will hang up their stethoscopes and those who are working extra shifts or multiple jobs will return to part-time status and/or resign one of their positions. When this happens, many communities will actually experience a nursing shortage and will be clamoring for nurses to work in their hospitals and other health care settings.

Continue to Believe in the Profession of Nursing!

Remind yourself of the reasons you chose nursing for your career. Some of you waited a year or more to be accepted into nursing school because there were more applicants than available educational slots. Don't forget the joy and enthusiasm you experienced the day you were accepted into nursing school!

You will experience that joy and enthusiasm again, when you land the nursing position that's right for you. It will continue as you grow in your career and experience the amazing opportunities available to you as a professional nurse.